REALITY AT RISK:

*A Defence of Realism
in Philosophy and the
Sciences*

HARVESTER STUDIES IN PHILOSOPHY

General Editor: Margaret A. Boden
Reader in Philosophy, University of Sussex

REALITY
AT RISK:

A Defence of Realism in Philosophy and the Sciences

ROGER TRIGG
Reader in Philosophy, University of Warwick

THE HARVESTER PRESS · SUSSEX

BARNES & NOBLE BOOKS · NEW JERSEY

First published in Great Britain in 1980 by
THE HARVESTER PRESS LIMITED
Publishers: John Spiers and Margaret A. Boden
16 Ship Street, Brighton, Sussex

and in the USA by
BARNES & NOBLE BOOKS
81 Adams Drive, Totowa, New Jersey 07512

© 1980, Roger Trigg

British Library Cataloguing in Publication Data

Trigg, Roger
   Reality at risk. -(Harvester studies in
   Philosophy; vol. 12).
   1. Realism
   I. Title
   149' .2   B835
   ISBN 0—85527—937—0

Barnes & Noble Books
ISBN 0–389–20037–9

Printed in Great Britain by
REDWOOD BURN LIMITED, Trowbridge and Esher

Contents

INTRODUCTION

The well-known story told by Boswell shows one response to Berkeley's denial of the existence of matter and his view that reality is dependent on mind. Dr Johnson said: 'striking his foot with mighty force against a large stone, till he rebounded from it, "I refute it *thus*" '. Yet idealism cannot be dismissed so easily, and it constantly reappears in different forms. The notion that what there is must somehow be dependent on someone being able to perceive it, conceive of it, or even describe it, remains a constant temptation, even though at first sight it does not accord with 'common sense'. I ended my *Reason and Commitment* by remarking: 'What in fact has been missing from so much recent controversy in religion, science and other fields, is the notion of objectivity – of things being the case whether people recognize them or not.' I said that what reality is like and how we conceive it are always separate questions. The purpose of this book is to argue that this view, realism, must indeed be the correct one.

There is a fundamental divergence between those who wish to 'construct' reality out of men's experiences, concepts, language or whatever, and those who start with the idea that what exists does so whether men conceive of it or not. Many forms of idealism or anti-realism are essentially anthropocentric. What is real is limited to what is real for men. Berkeley avoided this by including the mind of God in his theory. The Vienna Circle, on the other hand, was glad to emphasize the anthropocentric character of its empiricism. Its members, meeting in Vienna in the 1920s and early 1930s, rejected metaphysics and insisted in a pamphlet[1] that 'there is knowledge only from experience which rests on what is

vii

immediately given'. They insisted that 'something is "real" through being incorporated into the total structure of experience'. As they said, echoing Protagoras, 'everything is accessible to man; and man is the measure of all things . . . The scientific world-conception knows no unsolvable riddle'. Every statement which could not be reduced to the 'simplest statements about the empirically given' was dismissed as empty of meaning.

These attitudes of the Vienna Circle have permeated Anglo-American philosophy. Both W. V. Quine and A. J. Ayer attended meetings of the Circle and their writings show its influence. The Circle replaced the notion of objectivity with what can be grasped intersubjectively. 'Reality' became synonymous with the world of experience or 'the empirical world'. This was done in the name of science, and yet, as I shall argue, science itself demands a notion of a reality independent of men.

One physicist has argued[2] for what he terms 'a principle of ignorance' in the case of gravitational collapse which produces a black hole. He talks of a 'hidden surface', 'about which the observer can have only limited information such as the flux of energy, angular momentum, or charge'. He says that all data on this, compatible with the observer's limited information, are equally probable. In other words, the internal state of the black hole is in principle inaccessible. His conclusion is that 'gravitation introduces a new level of uncertainty or randomness into physics over and above the uncertainty usually associated with quantum mechanics'. He refers to Einstein's unhappiness about the unpredictability of quantum mechanics because he felt that 'God does not play dice.' Hawking's reply is that 'the results here indicate that God not only plays dice, He sometimes throws the dice where they cannot be seen'.

An empiricist would refuse to accept such talk of anything in principle unobservable, and, according to the outlook of the Vienna Circle, Hawking could not even state his theory in a meaningful way. The question is not whether he is right in his beliefs about black holes, but whether he can consistently even talk of a principle of ignorance. Can there be parts of reality from which man is in principle excluded? This is a conceptual question. Dice which are in principle unobservable may seem indistinguishable from the absence of any dice. The realist, however, starting from objective reality rather than man's knowledge of it, will not be surprised if some portions of it elude man's grasp for ever. He will insist that though this limits man's knowledge, it cannot affect the nature of what exists, since reality is self-subsistent. There does seem something strange indeed about a philosophical view which makes particular claim to be in tune with science and yet which cannot allow apparently respectable physical theories even to be stated. The trouble is that reality is far stranger than many versions of empiricism ever envisaged, and perhaps stranger than man *can* envisage. Yet it is impossible to assert this coherently if reality is in some sense a human construction.

Idealists have typically assumed that men are everywhere the same and that therefore a single reality will be constructed. This position becomes harder to maintain when human differences are emphasized and the considerable divergence between beliefs noted. This is particularly the case in some disciplines, and it is not surprising that in them the rejection of realism often degenerates into a relativism which not only makes what counts as real depend on man's judgements, but relates it to the judgements of particular societies or groups. As a result, 'reality' is only reality for a particular society and what is real and hence true for one set of people may not be for another. Social anthropology has been bedevilled by this kind of approach, so that some social anthropologists are tempted to talk of members of different cultures living in different worlds.[3] It is not surprising that understanding another culture becomes a major problem, and the very existence of social anthropology as a discipline is put in jeopardy.

Some sociologists have gone to surprising lengths in their

accounts of the 'social construction of reality'. Their difficulty has been that once it is admitted that all beliefs and theories are created by the social background, they have in all consistency to make this reflexive. Their own sociological insights have themselves to be seen as merely a particular group's constuction of reality. I shall refer to this again in the chapter on the sociology of knowledge. Ethnomethodology provides another example in the social sciences where emphasizing the social creation of reality can threaten the very discipline propounding the view. An extreme version[4] asserts that 'one of the principles of ethnomethodology is that objects are not constant, but instead are the creation of a ceaseless body of reality work'. Reality is thus made and not discovered, and there will be many alternative realities. We are told that 'one reality cannot investigate another without running it through its own knowledge and reasoning system'. This means that all social science, ethnomethodology included, is imprisoned within its own ways of thinking. Indeed it is asserted:[5] 'Ethnomethodology treats social science as one more reality among the many. It suggests that social science distorts other realities because it views them only through the lenses of its own system . . . The imposition of one reality on another necessarily distorts the reality studied.'

It is not surprising that it is freely admitted:[6] 'Ethnomethodology is not a method of pursuing the truth about the world. Rather it examines the many versions, including its own, of the way the world is assembled'. Readers of that may be forgiven for wondering why, if this is a correct account of the discipline, anyone should pay any attention to ethnomethodology. One method will not seem preferable to any other, if there are just different ways of constructing reality. Why, too, engage in social science, when it inevitably distorts the reality it purports to investigate? The repudiation of realism, in whatever context, can lead to a debilitating nihilism. Once one gives up any claim to be talking of how things are, but merely investigates how people judge that they are, or how one judges that they judge they are (and so on in an infinite regress), the rationale for whatever discipline one is engaging in disappears. This applies even in the social sciences where the social systems or cultures under investigation may themselves have been produced by men. It still remains true, according to realism, that the institutions, beliefs and so on being examined are logically independent of the investigator's conceptions of them.

There is often considerable disagreement between physical scientists, with many competing theories. Even though common sense would hold that there is one physical world, anyone stressing the human construction of reality would be tempted to hold that different scientific theories build up different worlds. This is a fairly common position and I shall pay particular attention to the physical sciences as a test case for realism. The work of such writers as Kuhn and Feyerabend in attacking empiricist views of science has done much in recent years to counteract the view of scientists as passive recipients of theory-neutral empirical data. They have emphasized the pre-eminent role of theory in science, to such an extent that even scientific theories are held to refer to different worlds. As a result, what counts as real is decided *within* a theory, and the theory does not appear to be about anything extra-theoretical. Questions as to how the adherents can ever understand a different one, and problems about why anyone should change from one theory to another must then be faced.[7] Kuhn, for example, finds it difficult to explain what 'scientific progress' is, as he has ruled out the possibility of new theories being nearer the truth.

Kuhn and Feyerabend make it seem very mysterious, if not impossible, that anyone should adopt one theory rather than another on rational grounds. Their accounts appear to invite the sociologist or the psychologist to give explanations why one theory was chosen. This shifts attention away from the content of belief to the mere fact of its being held. Questions about the nature of reality become replaced by questions why someone has a particular belief about it. This is a particular concern of the sociology of knowledge, and it is often coupled with an acceptance of determinism. I shall argue that this ultimately involves the removal of the possibility of rationality, so that we believe what we are caused to believe and it is a matter of chance if our belief is true.

One attraction of empiricism is the way it insists that our views about reality are built on incontestable, inter-subjective, repeatable data. It is a paradox that although private experience appears to form its shifting and insub-stantial base, its emphasis on intersubjectivity makes empiricism typically very preoccupied with what is publicly accessible. The result is that knowledge appears to be built on a solid foundation. This crumbles away, once anyone insists that empirical data are not neutral between theories, and that a theory determines which data are relevant (and even what is to count as a datum). Realism, on the other hand, makes objective reality, whether experienced or not, invariant between theories. This enables science to have a goal and gives a purpose to change from one theory to another, since our aim is to gain a fuller understanding of that reality.

Insisting that reality and our theories about it must be distinct means that ontological and epistemological ques-tions must always be kept separate. What there is and how we can know it are different issues. The reduction of the former to the latter is a typical result of empiricism. One writer on science, propounding a realist view, talks of what he calls the 'epistemic fallacy'[8] which, in his opinion 'consists in the view that statements about being can be reduced to, or analysed in terms of, statements about knowledge: i.e. that ontological questions can always be transposed into epistemological terms'. I agree that such a position is mistaken, and I shall try to show how even in the controversial case of quantum mechanics it is fatal to reduce talk of partially inaccessible particles to talk of measurements and observations. Bhaskar, however, wants to combine his realist position with a view of science as an ongoing social activity, with knowledge as a 'social product'. The trouble is that although ontology and epistemology may be distinct, ontology can easily be forgotten altogether once they are prised too far apart. I shall argue that although it is a truism that we cannot conceive of reality without conceiving of it, that does not mean that some of our conceptions may not be correct. We may not always know that they are, but that is a different question. Bhaskar, however, is very concerned with the problem of the relativity of our knowledge. Undue emphasis on the social conditioning of our beliefs in general or scientific theories in particular undoubtedly results in this kind of difficulty. He says[9] (and I shall deal with other versions of this view):

> Whenever we speak of things or of events etc. in science we must always speak of them and know them under particular descriptions, descriptions which will always be to a greater or lesser extent theoretically determined, which are not neutral reflections of a given world. Epistemological relativism, in this sense, is the handmaiden of ontological realism and must be accepted.

This argument always paves the way to various forms of conceptual idealism, and even relativism. Yet it is never explained why descriptions of the world should be neutral as between different theories. If one theory is correct and another mistaken, the world will be as the first theory says it is. The notion that we should be able to appeal to neutral data is a hangover from empiricism which demands that all theories should be deduced from a neutral body of experience. We do not, though, live in a 'neutral' world. It has a particular objective character, and the aim of scientific theories is to tell us what that is. The truism that we cannot know objects except under particular descriptions does not conflict with the view that some of these descriptions may be accurate. Bhaskar even says that epistemological relativism entails the rejection of any correspondence theory of truth. This suggests that the realism for which he argues eventually

gets forgotten, since a realist has to argue that statements
about the world have to reflect, or correspond with, that
world if they are to be true. Otherwise the 'world' becomes
totally irrelevant to questions of truth. Realism need not take
any position about the exact kind of correspondence re-
quired, but it must at least assert that true theories are true *in
virtue of* the nature of objective reality. Truth has its source in
reality, and as a consequence questions about the nature of
truth are distinct from those about the best way of reaching
it.

The source of Bhaskar's problem lies in an excessive
reaction from empiricism. Emphasizing that theories are not
built on a common empirical base, but determine what is to
count as real, can be an important step away from the
anthropocentric character of experience to a recognition that
theories are about reality, whether experienced or not.
Unfortunately, by repudiating the intersubjective character
of experience, this position may end up by turning to a
relativism which simply states that what is real is a matter
internal to theories, with no reason for preferring one theory
to another. This brings us back to the position advocated by
Kuhn and Feyerabend. What is needed is to replace intersubjectivity not with anarchy or a theory-based relativism,
but with the concept of objective reality.

The notion of 'constructing' reality rather than discovering it appears in many different disciplines. I shall deal with
sociological versions of it, but it is relevant to note that there
are also constructivist theories in psychology. Piaget, for
example, argues for what he calls 'genetic epistemology'
according to which the nature of knowledge cannot be
understood without reference to its origins, particularly
biological ones. He argues[10] that the genesis of cognitive
structures 'provides the constitutive conditions of knowledge'. He talks[11] of 'decentring', whereby the subject moves
away from his own subjectivity. The passage from childhood
to adulthood provides an example, but Piaget gives the
concept wider application. Indeed he says that 'the decentr-

ing of the subject and the construction of the object are two aspects of one and the same integrated activity'. He insists that 'the object is in the first instance only known through the subject's actions, and therefore must itself be constructed'. He adds that objects are constructed by a process of successive approximations, and represent 'a limit never itself attained'. For all practical purposes, therefore, objectivity is a construct of the individual's mind, although Piaget does conclude that 'objects certainly exist, and they involve structures which also exist independently of us'. Yet this concession is of vital importance since it means that there is *one* objective limit at which all subjects aim. Piaget, however, does not let it play a decisive role in the development of concept. The more that he emphasizes the construction of objects by individuals, the more inexplicable it is that they somehow construct the same ones. Even if biological factors are taken into account, there must still be some independent explanation why they lead to knowledge of reality. They must, too, presumably be themselves objective and not merely constructs by the biologist. Whereas the temptation of those who talk of the social construction of reality must always be relativism, that of those who deal with the individual's construction of it must be solipsism. Each person may construct his own world, with no overlap with that of others. Indeed other people would be merely his constructs.

Piaget has been criticized for seriously underestimating the social in his approach. Hamlyn[12] argues that other people alone can provide the context in which the concept of knowledge is applicable. He says: 'The concepts of know-ledge, truth and objectivity are social in the sense that they imply a framework of agreement on what counts as known, true and objective.' This is an intentional echo of the later Wittgenstein's position, and it is an attractive view for those who, like Wittgenstein, pay particular attention to language as a social phenomenon. Cannot agreement provide the basis for our conceptions of reality? For instance, one philosopher says:[13] 'If anything could be said to underline the non-arbitrary use of words and to make genuine classification possible, it is what Wittgenstein calls "agreement in judgements" and not "objective similarities".' He also says: 'The source of the objectivity of our judgements is language itself (and that brings in the way we live, act and re-act), and not anything independent of this'. I have discussed some of the unpalatable consequences of this kind of position in *Reason and Commitment*. It renders the teaching of language and translation between languages exceedingly problematic, since language is no longer understood as being *about* anything which can be grasped independently of it, and to which we all have access. Yet, language and the reality it attempts to describe must be logically distinct.

Since considerable disagreement exists between humans, emphasizing the importance of agreement can easily lead to the view that the parties to different sets of agreements live in different worlds. A leading philosopher of language, D. Davidson, attempts to avoid this by insisting on the assumption of a wide measure of agreement about the world by the speakers of different languages. This will, he thinks, ensure translatability, but he rules out the intelligibility of the notion of alternative conceptual frameworks. He is unable, too, to make the basic realist distinction between what is generally held true and what is true. Davidson has been influenced by Quine, and both consider that problems of interpretation and translation are more fundamental than questions of the relationship of language or scientific theory to reality. Reality cannot be approached except through our theories of it, and so Quine believes that no sense can be given to the notion of a reality totally independent of any theory. In this he is echoing the demand of the American pragmatist, Peirce, that we should start from where we are. Peirce believed that reality was what all scientists would one day agree about. I shall be discussing the ambiguities of this, but Quine does not accept that ultimately there could be one characterization of reality. Even when all possible data had been collected, alternative theories could still be adopted, and problems of translation between them would still remain.

Understanding other cultures became a theoretical problem for anthropologists when they lost their grip on the notion of objective reality. An analogous issue arises when philosophers of language lose sight of what language is about. Translation becomes a problem. Much of Davidson's work has been devoted to showing how we can interpret what the speakers of an alien language say, and this involves discovering a method for going from sentences of one language to sentences of another. The fundamental relationship to be discovered, according to Davidson, is that between the parts of one language with those of another, and not between words and objects. Objects can only be approached through a particular language. The notion of reference has often been invoked as the means by which words in a language pick out parts of reality, but Davidson rejects the view that sentences are built up from their parts. As a result, referring expressions can only be understood because of their role in sentences. He concludes[14] that 'there is no chance of explaining reference directly in non-linguistic terms'. This has the effect of removing attention from what a sentence is *about*, to the behaviour of the speaker of a strange language when he utters a sentence.

One advantage of an adequate theory of reference would be its firm hold on the notion of extra-linguistic reality. In one sense, Davidson is not denying the existence of a world beyond language which language is about, but it plays little part in his theory of interpretation. Other theories of reference, such as those of Kripke and Putnam, have attempted to show how even people with very different beliefs may still be talking about the same objects. A physicist could change his theory of electrons radically, and maintain he had been completely wrong about *them* before. He could be understood as referring to the same entities in both his earlier and later theories. What is picked out in the world by a theory is independent of the theory's truth. Indeed theories could not be mistaken unless they are about something independent of the theory.

Linked with questions concering reference are those concerning meaning, and realism has to face a particular problem about that, apart from the general question of the relationship of language as such and reality. Is the meaning of a sentence linked with the conditions under which we can verify its truth, or with the conditions under which it is true? Given this choice, the realist would wish to assert the latter, since truth must certainly not be tied to the anthropocentric concept of verification rather than to reality. Yet how can we know the meaning of a sentence, when we are not in a position to decide whether it is true or false? The problem is where the extra meaning comes from, if meaning has to be linked with truth conditions, and they outstrip verification conditions. One difficulty might then be that we cannot be fully aware of the meaning of what we say. It is perhaps not surprising that some philosophers try to avoid this by insisting on the anti-realist position that concepts gain their meaning from the conditions under which we acquire them. It is not part of my purpose in this book to give a detailed account of the relationship between meaning and truth. I merely insist that whatever theory of meaning is produced must do justice to the basic realist insights—that what is true is to be distinguished from what can be recognized as true, or what people agree is true, and that sentences can be true or false even when we have no means for finding out which is the case. This runs counter, for example, to the anti-realist views discussed by Dummett.

I shall deal particularly with scientific theories about reality, but I am not putting forward a 'scientific realist' view, and do not insist that reality should be limited to what is accessible to science and scientific method. It is hard to see how a realist could put such a prior restriction on the nature of reality without implicitly limiting reality at the outset to what man's science (and perhaps merely contemporary science) can comprehend. This is a first step back to an anti-realist anthropocentricity. I reject, too, the assumption made by many, including Lenin, that the terms 'realism' and 'materialism' are synonymous. The materialist may be correct to insist that material reality is the only reality, but that is an additional thesis, needing further argument. A realist can hold that material reality is not dependent on mind, without thereby denying the reality of anything non-material. Even a theist can assert a realist notion of God existing independently of men's conceptions of Him, and not espouse idealism, because he also accepts the independent reality of the material world.

Lenin thought that the fight between materialism and idealism was the fundamental dispute in the history of philosophy, and certainly it has been an explicit issue at least since the time of Plato. Lenin located atheism on one side and theism on the other, but clouded the issue by defining realism as materialism. Things are not so simple. Realism is a neutral doctrine about the character of what is real, and many brands of idealism merely insist on the dependence of reality on man's conceptions, without assuming the existence of God. Indeed some forms of empiricism (such as that of the Vienna Circle) can be both antirealist and avowedly atheist.

The dispute between realists and anti-realists is of vital importance in philosophy. The very fact that the same issue can reappear in so many different contexts is significant. The same controversy is bound to be relevant in *every* area where man's understanding of the world and his place in it is in question. Is *what* he understands distinct from his understanding of it? Do his concepts and language enable him to *discover* the world or even perhaps in some sense to *create* it? The physical scientist and the social scientist both have to grapple with the same problem, and the answer they give has a direct bearing on the purpose of their disciplines. Those philosophers who have emphasized the importance of man's experience and of verification may not think they are denying the reality of the 'external world'. They do, however, make it in some sense dependent on man by limiting it to what is accessible to him. Realism is opposed to this doctrine, in whatever guise it appears.

My own particular intellectual debts are too numerous to list. I would, however, like to mention special lectures given by Professor W. V. Quine and by Professor H. Putnam in Oxford, and by Professor J. A. Wheeler in London, Ontario. I found subsequent formal and informal discussion with them particularly helpful. I am also very grateful to Dr Margaret Boden and to Dr Michael Lockwood for their comments on an earlier draft of the book.

1 THE OBJECTIVITY OF REALITY

Reality and Mind

We cannot talk or think about reality without talking or thinking about it. This is a truism which seems almost too boring to bother about. We cannot have a conception of something without employing the conceptual scheme we have at our disposal. Yet this obvious point very often provides the starting point for major philosophical doctrines about the relationship between thought and reality, between what there is and what we think there is. Anyone who starts off with the twin notions of thought, or concepts, and reality, may think that the major problem is how we match the two. Our concepts are, we may think, like a vast jigsaw, and the object of the exercise is to fit them together, producing new ones if necessary, so that a picture is constructed which will exactly mirror reality. The snag is that it is normally possible to compare a jigsaw with the original on the box to make sure it is accurate. The relationship of our concepts to reality does not allow the same kind of comparison. To go back to our truism, there is no way of picturing reality without picturing it. We cannot conceptualize reality and then check the concepts we have produced against reality. It is self-defeating to attempt to think of reality as it exists beyond our thoughts. There is no way that we can somehow hold our concepts in suspense, while we compare them with reality.

Our analogy with a jigsaw puzzle is not intended to be a very close one, but we can see the difficulties which arise if the picture on the box is lost before the pieces are put together. There is no check beyond whether the pieces fit together. There might be only one way in which they can, but in the case of our concepts, the way we think, there are many

1

different permutations. There is an added complication in that conceptual schemes develop and change. We can produce new concepts and discard or modify old ones. Progress in science very often depends on our ability to do just that. It is as if we have to put a jigsaw puzzle together to form a recognizable picture without having any idea what the picture is to be and at the same time being able to make new pieces and change the shape of old ones. We might eventually produce the picture which the original jigsaw was intended to portray, but it might just as easily be a completely new one, and the product of our own imagination.

A similar dilemma faces us when we start to wonder about the status of the reality posited by our conceptual scheme. Does it correspond in major respects to what in fact exists, or is it merely in some way the product of man? If the latter, where does that leave 'reality'? We cannot talk about reality without conceptualizing, so perhaps our conceptualizing merely creates a 'reality' and does not reflect it. It is no very great step to saying that reality does not exist independently of our thoughts, if it cannot be identified apart from the way we think. The alternative seems to be to say that reality in itself, as opposed to how we can conceive it, is completely inaccessible. Yet there could be another possibility, namely that reality is as we now conceive it to be, even though it exists independently of our conceptions of it. The consequence of this would be to make us infallible. Is the world in fact just as we take it to be? The answer is even more obviously 'no' if we substitute 'universe' for 'world'. We are only too aware of our ignorance about many cosmic processes. There are surely galaxies of which we have no inkling. Moreover, it is very likely that we are mistaken in many of our scientific beliefs. Our present ones are unlikely to be immune from future modification, to judge by the necessity for past revisions of our scientific beliefs. It is exceedingly rash to equate reality with the views we happen to have at the moment.

We are back with our same old problem once we ignore

the lure of an easily won infallibility. It is not just our problem. The question of the relationship between anything originating from man such as thought, concepts, ideas, beliefs or just plain language on the one hand, and reality on the other has been one of the most basic and persistently troublesome problems confronting philosophy. Questions about the nature of truth are involved, since it is plausible to suggest that it is what corresponds to an independently existing reality. Questions about the nature of reality also arise immediately. Reality is in some sense mental and not material, if the mind which conceives it thereby produces it. On the other hand, it may not be too difficult to argue that mind is itself part of material reality, if an independent, material reality is merely reflected by a passive mind. It is all too easy in such a context to use blanket terms such as 'materialism', 'idealism' or 'realism'. So many different philosophical doctrines have appropriated these terms that their use often confuses rather than illuminates. There is the added difficulty that they are fairly commonly used in ordinary speech in quite different contexts. Nevertheless it is true, if not very enlightening, to say that we are in part concerned with the traditional dispute between realists and idealists. 'Realism' is here meant to indicate the view that reality exists independently of our conceptions of it, though it may coincide with them. 'Idealism' is the name of the view that what exists is dependent on mind. There are myriad forms of this kind of position, but it can typically be rather anthropocentric. Whereas the realist emphasizes the independence from man of much of reality, the idealist relates the reality of things very intimately to the way they are conceived, and appear to men.

We now encounter another persuasive philosophical theme, the connection between appearance and reality. How far is it possible to say that things are other than they appear to be? The same problem about the inaccessibility of reality comes up again. We would, it seems, have no evidence for saying that appearances are deceptive and that the reality underlying the appearances is very different, unless we have access to that reality. Yet access to it would involve its appearance to us under some guise or other. The very distinction between the two seems to give an open invitation to philosophers to discard the notion of reality and concentrate on appearance. What possible good is the concept of a reality which is so removed from man that he can never comprehend it? What he does grasp becomes appearance by definition, and so the more we discover, the further reality recedes from us. Locke's reference to substance as a substratum underlying all phenomenal qualities was very much like this. He called[1] anyone's notion of pure substance 'only a supposition of he knows not what support of such qualities'. It was not surprising that Berkeley wanted to cut it out completely. Undue concentration on appearances embraced by mind seems to make minds the arbiters of what there is. Reality then becomes a projection of mind, as indeed Berkeley's idealism made it. He saved his philosophy from being anthropocentric by making reference to God as well as to men's minds. Without God, idealism makes reality dependent on *man's* judgements. The dichotomy between appearance and reality can force us to choose between an inaccessible, and hence useless, reality, or an anthropocentricity which seems to say that things only exist as long as men think they do.

Another basic theme intertwined with these problems is the question of the active or passive nature of the mind. If there is a reality independent of our minds, one possible way our minds will come into contact with it is by being the passive recipients of information originating outside them. This is a typical empiricist view and has been caricatured by Sir Karl Popper as 'the bucket theory of the mind'. On the other hand, minds have a much more active role if reality is in some sense dependent on them. The world is in that case as the human mind portrays it as being. Our minds would not be constrained in any way but can, it seems, produce whatever reality they please. Such a notion of limitless

THE OBJECTIVITY OF REALITY

creativity is obviously a dangerous one. It would be very easy to say that *each* mind has it and before long one would be emmeshed in the incongruities of solipsism, with each mind producing its own world.

Some forms of idealism, such as those which refer to an 'Absolute', have been out of fashion for a long time, but the basic controversies which gave rise to realism or idealism are as alive as ever. There may not be many who would follow Berkeley in making the existence of things outside minds dependent on them. That is ontological idealism. Various forms of conceptual idealism are much more popular. They make the human mind, individually or collectively, the prime factor in the moulding of our concepts of reality, rather than any external 'reality'. Our concepts would not then be understood as an attempt to reflect things as they are, since it is alleged that to say they are one way rather than another is already to conceptualize them. Some writers may prefer to talk of the conceptual scheme presented by language rather than by mind, but the basic view in each case is that our understanding of reality is conditioned by *our* concepts and not by reality. In fact, according to a view like this, reality is (for us) an amorphous, unstructured chaos before it is conceptualized. There is no way we can apprehend reality directly without the mediation and enlightenment provided by whatever conceptual scheme we may have. Whether we have a choice of different conceptual schemes, or whether there is only one such scheme which we can have in virtue of our common humanity is another issue. It becomes an important one, once the close links between concepts and what is being conceptualized are broken.

Conceptual Idealism

An example of conceptual idealism is provided by the position argued by Nicholas Rescher. His idealism is explicit but he differentiates it from ontological idealism. He holds[2] that 'what the mind "makes" is not nature itself, but the mode-and-manner-determining categories in terms of which we conceive it'. He maintains: 'the mind shapes (rather than "makes" pure and simple) not nature itself, but nature as it is *for us*'. He insists that what is mind-dependent 'is not *reality itself* (whatever *that* might be) but reality-as-we-picture-it'. Almost nothing can be said about reality itself. Certainly individual things could not be understood to exist, since, according to Rescher,[3] 'objects must be thought of. . . from a perspective or point of view'. As he says,[4] 'concepts are used in all carving up of reality into distinguishable particulars'. What makes something what it is rather than something else depends on our conceptual scheme. The scheme determines what is to count as 'a thing', when one thing stops and another starts, and so on. Rescher faces the obvious objection that objects would still exist if there were no minds, and that many did exist before there were any. This kind of point is irrelevant to conceptual idealism, which is not concerned with ontology. The conceptual idealist is not going to be surprised by remarks about history. He will reply that he is not denying that rocks did not exist before men. He is only making the point that the very category of rock is not just 'read off' from the world, but is itself the product of mind. Rescher uses the example of the moon and agrees that in a sense it would exist even if there were no minds and never had been. As he puts it, 'the key question is just *what* it would be that would exist'. Answering 'the moon' is already to use a conceptual scheme. Rescher firmly maintains that a world without the process of mind-invoking conceptualization 'is a world in which there might generally be *existence* but to which the idea of particular existents would be inapplicable'. We would be left with a 'world without particulars: a night in which all cows are black'. Nothing could be distinguished, and hence, Rescher thinks, there would *be* no distinct things. A chair can only be specified relative to a framework of identification.[5] It only counts as a chair because of the conceptual perspective from which we are operating. There can be no sense in asking what the chair is really or objectively. One cannot subtract all perspectives and say what the chair is 'in itself'. Rescher would hold that this is not just because of the trivial point that we cannot say what it is in itself without operating from a particular perspective. The 'chair' does not exist independently of all perspectives. He says: 'Its identity, and so *it itself* as the specific individual it is, is perspective-restricted.'

When we think in terms of concepts and reality as two different sets of items, one produced by man and the other independent of him, and then try and fit them together, the perennial problem is how we can ever gain access to the second item. Rescher uses this to conclude[6] that 'reality-as-we-think-of-it (= our reality) is the only reality we can deal with'. As a result, everything of importance is included on the conceptual side of the dichotomy between concepts and reality. Reality itself becomes totally irrelevant. We must no longer think of it as being any help in the validation of our concepts or our establishment of truth. Rescher neatly points out[7] that any idea of our concepts corresponding or failing to correspond with reality is not very helpful. What 'reality' is being invoked here? If it is reality in itself construed in mind-independent terms, it has been defined in such a way that it is totally out of reach. If, on the other hand, it is reality-as-we-think-it, there is naturally a correspondence between that and the concepts we use to direct reality. Reality-as-we-think-it *is* reality already conceptualized by us and so it is already on the conceptual side of the barrier apparently set up between concepts and reality. Such a barrier inevitably creates problems. When we want to say any two items correspond, we need independent access to both in order to compare them. Because we never look at reality as it is, but only at reality as it appears to us, it will always be tempting to do as Rescher does and leave reality-in-itself on one side. He does not come to any conclusion about what there is. The same kind of argument might impel some to say that reality *is* just what we think it is. Rescher is content to make the conceptual point that we cannot talk or think of any reality independent of mind.

Such a view about the conceptual-dependence of our reality will always have important repercussions for our view of truth. The most natural view of truth involves the idea of correspondence with an independent reality. It is no exaggeration to say that this is the view of commonsense. Sentences, or propositions are true when they express what is in fact the case in the world. Rescher's view inevitably makes this an untenable account of truth, since it blocks access to 'the world' apart from our views about it. We are kept very firmly on one side of the correspondence relation and are in principle stopped from examining the other side. Doing so would involve conceptualizing reality and this brings us back to the conceptual side of the fence. Reality 'in the raw' is thus blocked off forever from view. Rescher accepts this conclusion and advocates a coherence theory of truth. He says: 'As we have no theory-independent apprehension of reality, the best we can possibly do is to construct a coherent conceptual and theoretical scheme *about* reality.' Without the possibility of correspondence to 'extra-theoretical facts' or unconceptualized reality, it seems that we can only make our beliefs as coherent as we can. Views about the accessibility of reality must affect our conceptions of the nature of truth.

It might seem that all Rescher is concerned about is the epistemological impossibility of stepping out of our beliefs to check them. He wants to argue for an even stronger conclusion. Our concepts are not appropriate as mere descriptions of a mind-independent reality, because they are themselves mind-invoking. This raises the question again of the status of the reality which is always inaccessible to us. Is it merely an unknowable something-or-other? When Wittgenstein was concerned about the relationship between the concept of pain and the reality of pain, he concluded[8] that 'a "nothing" would serve just as well as a something about which nothing could be said'. Is a reality about which nothing can be said, no better than no reality at all? Wittgenstein was writing about the reality of sensation, but applying his remarks more widely could involve accepting ontological idealism, and holding that the only reality is our *thought* of what exists. Apart from the assault on common sense which such a position makes, it runs into very great diffeculties when it has to account for such phenomena as scientific discovery or scientific progress. *What* is being discovered? *What* are scientists investigating? *How* does knowledge increase? It is exceedingly puzzling why scientists should ever change their minds or think anything different, if there is nothing real apart from their thoughts. Rescher attempts to avoid this kind of problem by concentrating on the nature of concepts and their relation to mind. He insists that he is not a phenomenalist and denies[9] that 'the reality and persistence of physical objects inheres in the fact that human experiences occur regularly in certain systems'. He maintains that, unlike phenomenalism, conceptual idealism is not saying anything about 'the structural nature of reality'. 'We have', he says, 'no reason to deny the causal primacy of the reality postulated in our scientific theorizing regarding the nature of the world—a primacy which, from the internal perspective of scientific theory, is altogether absolute.' He thinks that our theorizing itself is incvitably mind-involving. Scientists, it seems, need not doubt the reality of what they are investigating, and science can tell us what exists. It is just that this has to be articulated in terms of a conceptual scheme. He says:[10]

> The conception of an altogether mind-independent reality is not self-contradictory, but is an essentially empty idealization. It leads along an ontological *via negativa*. . . We arrive at no conceptually stable terminus, but only at something of which we know that we can know nothing of it in terms of our conceptual scheme.

The question remains whether, despite his protestations, Rescher can really avoid the pitfalls of ontological idealism. Where mind-independent reality is by definition beyond reach, and we are only concerned with 'reality-for-us', and when our basic conceptual categories are imposed on the world rather than function as descriptions of independent processes, what point is there referring to any mind-independent reality? Wittgenstein's remark echoes in our ears. A reality we can know nothing of is not so very different from no reality at all. Ockham's razor gets specially sharpened by philosophers to deal with that kind of superfluous entity. One difficulty has probably been the way the problem has been set up. Once we distinguish between concepts and reality and realize that only conceptualized reality is accessible, unconceptualized reality is left with a metaphysical role which seems positively abhorrent to modern minds afraid of any truck with 'The Absolute' or such-like entities. It is no exaggeration to say that it was the kind of idealism that dealt with 'The Absolute' which encouraged the rise of logical positivism and the emphasis on verification through experience.

Rescher's insistence on how things are seen from the internal perspective of science certainly points to what is undeniably important. A scientist has to think that he is investigating something independent and is not just playing around with his own thoughts. The problem of the comparison between conceptual schemes and reality seems to threaten this. Once we make reality a shadowy something-or-other always blocked from view, the scientist is made to look as if his concern is with the mere positing of entities. Rescher's concern with the role of mind has made him underestimate the role of reality. Why, for instance, should reality always be blocked off by a conceptual scheme? Why may it not actually be as it is said to be? Concepts could be a window on reality, rather than a barrier to it. The obvious rejoinder is that even if this is so, it is impossible to know when it is. Knowing that a world beyond a window is as we see it through the window presupposes that we can go outside and see it for ourselves. It may be alleged that if we cannot, we are in no position to be sure that we are not, for instance, looking at a screen on which images are being projected. The problem is then transposed from ontology to epistemology. We are no longer concerned with what there is, but with how we can know what there is, and perhaps with how we can know that we know. Talking of ontology apart from epistemology may make some people reach for Ockham's razor again, but it will be a basic theme of this book that the two are separate. What there is in no way depends on how we can come to know it. Epistemology can be accommodated within talk about conceptual schemes: ontology cannot. Yet some might allege that ontology is itself theory-dependent. What we say exists is only what *we* say exists. Idealism typically links the ontological and epistemological. It hints that the objects of our knowledge depend in some crucial way on their being known, and refuses to acknowledge a gap between what exists and our knowledge of it.

The spectre of scepticism is a prime motivating force behind many idealist theories. Berkeley himself called[11] the belief in any reality apart from its being perceived 'the very root of scepticism'. His argument was that as long as men thought of real things existing outside the mind, and of knowledge as being real only so far as it was 'conformable to real things', they could not be certain they had any real knowledge at all. 'For', he asks trenchantly, 'how can it be known that the things which are perceived are conformable to those which are not perceived, or exist without the mind?' His conclusion was that 'unthinking beings perceived by sense have no existence distinct from being perceived'. This was certainly a reduction of ontology to epistemology with a vengeance. The problem posed by Berkeley is the one presented by all idealists. The impossibility of any independent knowledge about reality which could be produced to confirm the knowledge we already have, could easily provoke scepticism. There are two responses to the problem. One is to say that there is no such thing as 'reality'. There are only men's beliefs. The other path avoids such outright scepticism, but claims that reality is the product of belief. Although we cannot skirt round our beliefs to check them against reality, we can, as Rescher points out, systematize them and check them against each other. The result is a coherence theory of truth, and a view of 'reality-for-us'.

Any radical break between beliefs and reality, or concepts and reality, seems to make 'reality' inaccessible and totally mysterious. The response to the problem is at root the same, whether the existence of things is made to depend in some way on our perception of them or their 'thinghood' is decided by the conceptual scheme we have. Reality is reduced to 'reality-for-us'. The world becomes anthropocentric. In many respects, this is similar to Kant's so-called 'Copernican revolution'. Copernicus had established that the spectator was going round the heavenly bodies rather than vice-versa. Because the earth was not the centre of the universe, the explanation of observations of the sun going round lay with the situation of the spectator and not with the object itself. Kant[12] thought that a similar approach to the problem of the relationship between concepts and objects might be fruitful. He says: 'Hitherto, it has been assumed that all our knowledge must conform to objects. . . We must make trial whether we may not have more success in the tasks of metaphysics, if we suppose that objects must conform to our knowledge.'

Whilst Kant thought that our categories of thought had their origin in men rather than in any external objects, it is notorious that he still made room for what he termed 'noumena', things in themselves, as opposed to objects of the senses, or appearances. He says:[13] 'Our understanding. . . sets limits to itself, recognizing that it cannot know these noumena through any of the categories, and that it must therefore think them only under the title of an unknown something.'

Like Locke's substance, Kant's 'things-in-themselves' have frightened off many philosophers. His distinction between appearances, regarded as representations, and the unknown things-in-themselves behind appearances parallels the dichotomy between concepts and reality, which we have already seen drawn by Rescher. It inevitably invites philosophers to jettison what they regard as the inaccessible second term of a bogus relationship. Tough-minded philosophers of an empiricist disposition have no use for such apparently useless entities.

Peirce's 'Final Agreement'

A very typical response came towards the end of the nineteenth century from C. S. Peirce, the American pragmatist. He tried to bridge the gap between beliefs and reality by cutting out any 'incognizables' and starting from people's beliefs. The meaningfulness of referring to things existing outside the comprehension of men will always be one of the main issues in any discussion of reality. Whatever we wish to count as 'things', many of them may lie outside our comprehension, if they exist independently of man's conception. It makes a difference whether they are thought to be inconceivable in principle, or whether they still lie outside men's understanding as a matter of empirical fact. Peirce made plenty of room for the latter, because he did not make reality correspond to men's present beliefs. He introduced the notion of a final agreement, when everyone would agree on what there is. Reality is quite simply for him what corresponds to this ultimate agreement. In this way, he made reality accessible, and linked it to men's beliefs. They are not necessarily our present beliefs but can be beliefs that will be arrived at one day.

Peirce is attempting to link the insights of realism with those of idealism. He refuses to countenance a break between the world and men's judgements about it. We shall see the world as it really is, when the scientific millennium arrives and complete agreement is reached. Peirce claims[14] that 'everything which will be thought to exist in the final opinion is real, and nothing else'. He says triumphantly that this theory of reality 'is instantly fatal to the idea of a thing in itself—a thing existing independent of all relation of the mind's conception of it'. Reality and our conception of it will in the end perfectly coincide. He maintains the following:

> All human thought and opinion contains an arbitrary, accidental element, dependent on the limitation in circumstances, power and bent of the individual; an element of error in short. But human opinion universally tends in the long run to a definite form, which is the truth. Let any human being have enough information and exert enough thought upon any question, and the result will be that he will arrive at a certain definite conclusion, which is the same that any other mind will reach under sufficiently favourable circumstances.

There is an optimism here about human rationality which may not seem very plausible to some. Peirce's general strategy is clear enough. He wants to hold to a realist view of truth while not getting encumbered with embarrassing metaphysical entities. The snag is that the final agreement seems to provide an ideal limit to enquiry other than an actual, foreseeable historical event. There is no guarantee that such an ultimate agreement will ever be reached, and it is difficult to give much sense to the idea of an actual agreement, if scientific investigation has to be infinitely prolonged. Peirce later modified his views on this. He wrote[15] towards the end of his life that 'truth's independence of individual opinions is due (so far as there is any "truth") to its being the predestined result to which sufficient enquiry *would* ultimately lead'. The use of the word 'would' indicates that the end of all enquiry has become a hypothetical matter and not a definite future event. Peirce's difficulty arises from the basic weakness of his whole approach. He is trying to bring together the concept of an ultimate agreement, which is problematic enough in itself, with that of reality. If he thinks that there are two separate items, there seems little reason to suppose that they should ever coincide completely, unless their coalescence is made true by definition. 'Final agreement' could be that which coincides with what is really the case. This would involve an appeal to reality beyond all agreement, and in fact the ultimate agreement, as opposed to some accidental agreement, would be defined by the reality.

This sometimes seems implicit in what Peirce says. For instance, he remarks:[16] 'It is unphilosophical to suppose that with regard to any given question (which has any clear meaning) investigations would not bring forth a solution of it, if it were carried far enough.' Apart from the fact that Peirce has no grounds, beyond mere prejudice, for an assertion like this, we must ask what he means by 'far enough'. He accepts that men are fallible and may sometimes agree about what is in fact false. Truth is not the outcome of any chance agreement, but is the result of persistent scientific investigation. When will that have been carried 'far enough'? An obvious answer left to Peirce, it seems, is when men see reality as it is. Even if he wanted to say that the agreement must be firm, and that investigation has been carried far enough when men no longer change their minds and are unassailed by doubt, he still has to face the risk that still further investigation may create new disagreement and sow new seeds of doubt.

Peirce is much more likely to have preferred to have defined reality via the agreement, rather than the final agreement by reality. After all, he may have wondered, if you have agreement, what more could you want? This seems to accord with his pragmatic viewpoint, but there is a definitely idealist slant to the view. How far is reality independent of the final agreement, and how far is it created by it? The fact that Peirce also suggests[17] that 'we cannot know there *is* any truth concerning any given question' indicates that we do have to wait for an agreement which may or may not occur. In other words, the agreement somehow constitutes the truth.

One of Peirce's basic maxims was 'Dismiss make-believes'.[18] He wanted nothing to do with superfluous entities, and wanted to come down to the concrete. He had no use for concepts without practical relevance. He claims:[19] 'There is a general *drift* in the history of human thought which will lead it to one general agreement, one catholic consent. And any truth more perfect than this destined conclusion, any reality more absolute than what is thought in it, is a fiction of metaphysics.'

A shift of emphasis from truth to what is believed true is evident here. Peirce is only concerned with men and their beliefs. He has no use for 'truth' or 'reality' in isolation from men and their judgements. In the same passage he enlarges on what he means by the catholic consent 'which constitutes the truth'. He says: 'It is by no means to be limited to men in this earthly life or to the human race, but extends to the whole communion of minds to which we belong, including some probably whose senses are very different from ours.'

This immediately makes such consent a mere hypothetical thing. An agreement between men in this life and men in some other one, perhaps even after death, or between men on this planet and beings with different perceptual equipment elsewhere, seems a fairly metaphysical concept in itself. As an actual historical event, or even a conceivable one, such an agreement seems pretty unlikely. How would one ever know when it had been reached? The sceptical problem about how we can ever know that we have arrived at truth or that our judgements coincide with reality is no different from how we can recognize 'catholic consent'. Peirce has brought in too many groups. It is very difficult to give any sense to consent once we talk of the possibility of different beings elsewhere, even if we ignore any implications in what Peirce says about a life after death contrasted with this earthly life. When there is agreement amongst all the beings we are acquainted with, how can we be sure that this is the ultimate agreement? There may be many other races of creatures with minds like ours on planets yet to be discovered, who totally disagree with us. If the answer is that the agreement merely sets an ideal limit, and is of no practical use, then it gets into precisely the predicament an independent reality would be in. It may act as a kind of goal or regulative principle but it can be very remote from men's actual beliefs. This is exactly what Peirce objects to. In an article on 'What Pragmatism is' he puts forward a view of truth which would find favour with many today. He said:[20]

> You only puzzle yourself by talking of this metaphysical 'truth' and metaphysical 'falsity' you know nothing about. All you have any dealings with are your doubts and beliefs. . . If by truth and falsity you mean something not definable in terms of doubt and belief in any way, then you are talking of entities of whose existence you can know nothing, and which Ockham's razor would clean shave off. Your problem would be greatly simplified if, instead of saying that you want to know the 'Truth', you were simply to say that you meant to attain a state of belief unassailable by doubt.

The shift from 'truth' to what is held true is a very typical one in modern philosophy. It is perfectly proper *if* it makes no sense to refer to a reality beyond our beliefs. There is, though, an important distinction to be made here. Peirce was impatient with concepts that were of no practical use, and a view of truth as correspondence to reality seems to be precisely in this position, however it may be spelt out. It is of little help to a scientist to be told that what he says is true if it tallies with what is the case. He is given no criteria to enable him to choose between competing viewpoints. The nature of truth is an insufficient guide if I am searching for what is true. I still have to find the best path. A footballer may know the rules of the game and what constitutes a goal, but he still has to learn the skill necessary for playing the game. A mere recital of the rules will not help him to shoot a goal. Epistemology is in many ways attempting to provide men with the means of sifting the true from the false, just as a coach may try and teach the skills and tactics necessary for winning games. Nevertheless the game would have no point without its rules. A game would become a series of unrelated, though doubtless clever, manoeuvres, without goals and the notion of winning and losing. It would degenerate into a bunch of men running up and down a restricted patch of ground. In the same way, epistemology without a goal, leaves a series of clever gambits with no ultimate point. This is the reason why the concept of truth is not an idle one even if truth seems inaccessible. Without a grip on reality, epistemology can degenerate very quickly.

Truth can always be seen from two points of view, that of the seeker of truth, whether a scientist or not, and that of the philosopher seeking a definition of truth and trying to establish the nature and status of reality. There is no doubt that philosophic definitions of truth are not particularly helpful to anyone trying to find out *what* is true. A physicist may be faced with two competing theories and has to decide what entities he will admit as real. Whether the decision is right may depend on whether what he says is so, but he needs a criterion to assist him. Being told that the nature of truth lies in the correspondence of propositions with reality will make him none the wiser.

Much philosophic discussion has been vitiated by the fact that the two viewpoints have not been adequately distinguished. Philosophers who want epistemological criteria in their pursuit of truth are going to be rather scornful of any reference to an inaccessible reality. Peirce was in this position. As a consequence, he emphasized the fact that one should start from where one is rather than entertain any abstract notion of truth.

He said:

> There is but one state of mind from which you can 'set out', namely the very state of mind in which you actually find yourself at the time you do 'set out' —a state in which you are laden with an immense mass of cognition already formed. . . Now that which you do not at all doubt, you must and do regard as infallible, absolute truth.

Everyone must start somewhere, and all this may be sound advice, if it is construed as advice on epistemological tactics. Talking of 'metaphysical' truth and falsity does not help someone who still has a long road to travel to reach it. To take our analogy with football again, it may not be very helpful merely to inform someone that the aim of the game is to shoot goals, when he has the ball at his feet at the wrong end of the field. Yet that aim is of paramount importance. Referring to a reality independent of men's conceptions of it may not help men's quest for it. The pursuit of knowledge without the existence of such a reality is like a game of football without the purpose that scoring goals gives it.

Objectivity and Intersubjectivity

Questions about the nature of truth are distinct from those about the best way of reaching it. Demands for a view of truth which is 'useful' to those who are searching for it are rather beside the point. Once we take human fallibility seriously, we cannot rest our views about truth on what men think is true. It would be like guessing the rules of football while watching two teams who play it so haphazardly that they never get to scoring goals. Yet the pursuit of truth underlies much human activity. To understand what a bad team is up to, it may be necessary to know what they are *trying* to do. We need to know of the possibility of truth *before* we see what men happen to believe. Indeed that alone gives belief its point.

It could be argued that the splitting of the nature of truth from our criteria is rather dangerous. Whether our tests for truth involve a demand for coherence amongst our beliefs, for some kind of final agreement, or for anything else, they are not directly connected with truth's nature. Does this mean that in the end our tests for truth are separated from truth itself? Peirce's notion of a final agreement, however remote, might provide us with a test for truth. If we insist that the nature of truth is unconnected with any such agreement, we have to face the possibility that we reach agreement and yet still be mistaken. Truth may still escape our grasp. Yet truth and the reality which true beliefs and statements are about seem inaccessible if our criteria for truth fail us, whether they be taken jointly or individually. Once more scepticism gains an entrance. We seem to be in trouble, when the problem is stated baldly like this. Yet the tests for truth, whatever they may be, actually guarantee truth, if the reverse is true. This would be natural, if they themselves constitute truth. Coherence is a sure guide when the coherence of beliefs or statements is what makes them true. Agreement can be relied on when what we *mean* by truth is what is finally agreed. The search for an infallible route to truth involves linking it logically with truth. Yet tests for truth are instruments used by *men* and designed for them. This inevitably means that truth and the reality described by the true statements men make become anthropocentric.

The natural consequence of insisting that reality is self-subsistent, not necessarily depending for its existence on human thought or language, is to make a break between truth and our tests for it. We are not infallible and neither is any criterion of truth we may have to hand. There must, though, be some link between a test for truth and the nature of reality. For instance, Peirce's view of the importance of a final agreement rests on a rather starry-eyed notion that we are always wholly rational. He supposes that everyone will inevitably come to the same correct conclusion given enough time for investigation and enough evidence. When he couples this with a dismissal of anything 'incognizable', he thinks that agreement guarantees truth and that reality is nothing more than whatever men will ultimately agree about. The notion of men's opinions converging with reality involves a deliberate balancing act. Reality can become the *product* of agreement and depend ontologically on it, or the agreement can be made so hypothetical that it is totally useless in practice. In fact, any realist would accept that there is a general connection between reality and what a rational man *would* accept as true if he had enough evidence. The snag is that the hypothetical would have to be interpreted very hypothetically in some cases and it would be difficult to prevent 'incognizables' reappearing in a way abhorrent to Peirce.

Reality can be envisaged from two sides. One is the epistemological side. Our striving for knowledge and our searching for firm criteria for judging what is true make many philosophers look to the possibility of agreement. We start from where we are and set ourselves an aim. We can see, though, that our judgements may miss the mark, however earnestly we strive, if we abstract ourselves from our present position in the way in which Peirce thinks meaningless. A thing is not so merely because we think it. This is to view things from an ontological point of view. Needless to say, we are not ourselves ever in a position to say of any given present belief that it is false. This would involve us thinking that what we still think is true is false. We think it true, if we think it true, and we cannot step out of ourselves in any way. There will, therefore, always be pressure to leave these realms of speculation. It will be argued that truth is an empty notion apart from the possibility of agreement, and that we should be content to make some sort of agreement our aim.

Another way of putting this kind of problem is in terms of the slippery concepts of subjectivity and objectivity. What is objectively so for the realist is what has some kind of independent existence. Men's social relations may not exist wholly apart from men. They obviously cannot. Even here, though, it is true to say that they could have existence apart from men's conception of them. This fact provides a footing for some writers on the social sciences for the concept of false consciousness. In contrast, many would be content to say in a variety of areas that intersubjective agreement provides all the objectivity one can get. The emphasis will depend on whether one is concentrating on possible epistemological criteria or talking more metaphysically about reality. Epistemologists generally wish to look for a contrast to an individual's judgements. What is necessary to avoid solipsism? One obvious answer is the admission of the existence of other people and the willingness to compare one's own judgement with theirs, and if necessary to be corrected by them. This is roughly what happens with everyday perceptual judgements. If I say that I see a cow in a field and other observers, including some who are nearer to the supposed object, deny that there is one there, I am unlikely to pursue my claim. I certainly thought I saw a cow, but I could easily have been taken in by a cloud shadow. We accept intersubjective agreement as a standard in such cases. Subjective experience can thus be contrasted with what is held true by common agreement. 'Subjective' can be the opposite of 'intersubjective' rather than 'objective'. To put it another way, the word 'objective' can refer in a weak sense to what is agreed on, rather than in a strong sense to what is 'really' the case.

The anti-realist will naturally prefer to emphasize the necessity for intersubjective agreement. It is however worth asking how far *anyone* can be a consistent anti-realist. How can anyone refuse to accept that 'things' do not exist independently of my conceptions? He can deny the meaningfulness of referring to anything beyond the reach of man, although the more hypothetical man's reach is made, the more positions of realist and anti-realist begin to coalesce. Yet a major hurdle will not be so much the existence of material objects as that of other minds, if the anti-realist starts from the standpoint of one man's judgements. Forms of idealism, emphasizing the priority of the mental over the material, will find this a particularly acute problem. I am in great danger of solipsism if other minds only exist in so far as I judge them to exist. Philosophers who start with the reality of mind are usually trying to convince other minds of the validity of what they say. It will, to say the least, be uncomfortable for them if they appear to be denying the independent reality of the minds they are addressing. An extreme subjectivism, denying the independent reality of anything beyond my judgements, rules out any ontology. It may say that only I exist, but there is even here a realist whiff to the claim. Am I saying that I exist independently of and prior to my judgements that I do? Very few would wish to start plumbing the depths of solipsist absurdity. Anti-realists are inevitably forced, if they conceive the problem in terms of the opposition of mind and matter, to admit the independent reality of other minds. Their reality must amount to far more than is conferred by my judgements about them. Idealism inevitably becomes objectivist, even when 'objectivist' is understood in its strong sense.

Epistemological realism is sometimes distinguished from the ontological sort, so that one can be an epistemological realist and an ontological idealist. In that case, only minds would exist, but there would be an external world beyond our judgements. What we know would be in no way dependent on our knowing it, but the reality which is the source of knowledge would be ultimately mental. This means that reality is not ultimately independent of judgement as such. It may be unconnected with what you think or what I think, but it is not unconnected with all minds. The 'incognizables' ruled out by Peirce would also be anathema to any ontological idealist. The latter will say that only minds are real, or at least that the material world is dependent on mind in some way. He might even hold that matter is in some sense a manifestation of mind.

In fact 'epistemological realism' is not a particularly surprising doctrine, for the simple fact that the only alternative to it is solipsism. Epistemological realism is the inevitable consequence of accepting that the world is not one's own creation, and that as a result one may be mistaken about its nature. Very few philosophers would consciously wish to be solipsists, even if their opponents may allege that this is what they are. Epistemological realism is then going to be part of the outlook of just about any philosopher. It is certainly a precondition of epistemology, since all the main epistemological problems simply disappear if I am merely creating my own world, rather than making discoveries about a world which exists apart from my own judgement.

There is scope for the introduction of a correspondence theory of truth once a gap has been opened between my judgements and what is the case. They may or may not correspond with reality, even one created by other men's minds. It is very often assumed that idealist theories of truth have to depend on coherence, while the notion of correspondence has to entail realism. This is too simple. The correspondence is thought to hold exclusively between, say, mind on the one hand and independent facts on the other. Yet this need not always be so. There is obviously room for the notion of correspondence between my judgements and facts which are independent of me, but not of minds in general. In such an instance, a correspondence theory of truth does not entail the existence of any independence reality. Idealism therefore is not inevitably going to reject correspondence in favour of coherence in its account of truth. The real thrust of the argument between an idealist and a realist is over the question of the status of extra-mental reality. This typically involves the issue of whether there can be anything which is inconceivable to man.

Peirce was certainly an epistemological realist, and at first sight some of the things he says might suggest that he was a fully-fledged one. For instance, he says:[21]

> You certainly opine that there is such a thing as Truth. Otherwise reasoning and thought would be without a purpose. What do you mean by there being such a thing as Truth? You mean that something is So — is correct or just — whether you, or I, or anybody thinks that it is so or not.

This may seem at variance with what Peirce says about the meaninglessness of metaphysical truth, but in fact it is consistent with his refusal to accept that anything is beyond the thought of men. In one of the passages in which he talks of the 'final opinion' he says[22] that it is 'independent not indeed of thought in general, but of all that is arbitrary and individual in thought: is quite independent of how you, or I, or any number of men think'. The 'Truth' which is so whether anybody thinks it or not, need not, in his view, be independent of thought as such. My thoughts may not tally or 'correspond' with what is ultimately the final opinion. It is quite proper to say that truth is independent of my thoughts or of any other individuals. Peirce does not think that reality is independent of what all men think at *any* time. His epistemological realism does not become ontological. My thoughts may be differentiated from those of the community of mankind, understood very abstractly, but the reality mankind thinks about is not clearly distinguished from their thoughts about it. There are times, particularly when he makes the final agreement hypothetical, when Peirce's attempts to link reality with thought would be acceptable to a realist. In the last resort, however, Peirce does not wish to make reality distinct from what men do, or at least can, think. What is must make itself manifest. Peirce's so-called 'realism' in the end can become what he terms 'objective idealism', whereby material objects themselves take on the nature of mind. He says that 'everything we can in any way take cognizance of is purely mental'. This makes it very clear that realism as an epistemological thesis can coexist with idealism as a thesis about the nature of reality.

Peirce's realism does not, as he puts it, 'sunder existence out of the mind and being in the mind as two wholly improportionable modes'. He says of the realist's position:[23]

> 'When a thing is in such relation to the individual mind that mind cognizes it, it is in the mind; and its being so in the mind will not in the least diminish its external existence. For he does not think of the mind as a receptacle, which if a thing is in, it ceases to be out of. . . The immediate object of thought in a true judgement *is* the reality.'

This is all completely acceptable. It implies a correspondence theory of truth, and states what must be presupposed by any doctrine of ontological realism. The mind can grasp reality as it is, without in any way lessening the objectivity (in a strong sense) of that reality. The whole point of realism is indeed that men conceive of reality without in any way making it dependent on their thought. The crucial question is the objectivity of the reality to which our thoughts correspond. It fails to be genuinely objective if it is conceptually linked to human judgements. Peirce's dislike of abstract entities, far removed from what men think, leads him to see the world in wholly anthropocentric terms. Reality apart from belief becomes mere 'metaphysical fiction' and 'make-believe' for him. At one point he mentions with approval the fact that physicists make the existence of the objects of their research depend 'upon their manifestation or rather on their manifestability'. He continues:[24] 'We have only to extend this conception to all real existence and to hold these two facts to be identical, namely that they exist and that sufficient investigation would lead to a settled belief in them to have our Idealistic theory of metaphysics.'

Peirce probably means here by 'Idealistic' no more than 'phenomenalistic', but no passage could illustrate more clearly the limits of his realism.

2   REALISM VERSUS ANTI-REALISM

The Distinction between Materialism and Realism

Realism is a theory about 'strong objectivity'. Intersubjective agreement cannot determine what there is. Idealism is opposed to this on the grounds that it opens a gap between men and reality which can only encourage scepticism. We seem trapped inside a conceptual world of our own construction if reality lies out of reach somewhere beyond our conceptual scheme. One solution is to relate the conceptual world logically to 'the world'. Various forms of idealism typically do just that and realism and idealism are for this reason typically thought to be opposites. The distinction noted between epistemological and ontological realism does not substantially affect this basic point. It just has to be made clear that idealism is opposed to ontological realism. What there is may include men's conceptions of the world, but the ontological realist will hold that it covers many other items, including whatever those conceptions, when accurate, are conceptions of. He may not deny the reality of mind and mental events, but would emphasize that everything cannot be reduced to them. Epistemological realism merely points to the externality of what I know. My thoughts do not constitute reality, and I can have knowledge of other minds and of whatever is dependent on mind for its reality. This is irrelevant to the larger question of the relationship between mind and reality, and the word 'realism' will be generally used to mean ontological realism. Needless to say, ontological realism entails epistemological realism, and arguments for the latter are also relevant for the former, although the ontological realist will feel that they do not establish enough.

There is a difference of emphasis between realism and

idealism, which may partly account for their different views. Idealism starts with what men know and attempts to work out from that. Realism tends to start from the opposite direction. It assumes the existence of reality, and then investigates men's place in that reality, and tries to explain how knowledge can arise. The awkward fact that we cannot talk of reality, except in very abstract terms, without already talking from the standpoint of man's knowledge, is of course precisely what gives ammunition to the idealist.

'Realism' is a neutral doctrine when it comes to defining the *character* of reality. All realism does is to protect the status of reality by denying that it is dependent on mind, concepts or language. Reality is not produced by man in any way and it is wrong, according to the realist, to describe reality in anthropocentric terms. There is, however, a large trap awaiting anyone who too readily assumes that idealism and realism are the obverse and reverse of the same coin. It is certainly impossible to espouse both at once. Idealism, though, says that the real is mental or dependent on mind. It is obviously fallacious to assume that anyone who denies this says that nothing real is mental or dependent on mind. It is perfectly open to realists to say that minds are real, but that they are not the only real things.

Although realists may be materialists, they do not have to be. The nature of the ultimate constituents of the world is a totally different problem from the relation of reality to our true judgements about it. Indeed realists leave open what is to be meant by 'the world'. We have used the term rather broadly to mean 'what there is'. The realist can accept that mind, matter and even other kinds of entities might exist. His argument with the idealist is not concerned with the reality of mind. He is merely concerned to hold that the mental does not exhaust reality.

A refutation of idealism may establish realism, rather than materialism. Similarly some arguments against idealism might establish materialism and not just realism. Although idealism rules out both theories, the two are far from being synonymous. For this reason, it will probably be less confusing subsequently if arguments opposed to the realist position, as we portray it, are dubbed simply anti-realist, rather than idealist. Other philosophic positions, very distinct from idealism, may yet be anti-realist. This is all far from being terminological quibbling. In his book *Materialism and Empirio-Criticism*, Lenin made a devastating attack on idealism, and claimed that the only alternative was *materialism*. He says[1] 'The fundamental principle of materialism is the recognition of the external world, and the existence of things outside our mind and independent of it.' Yet if this is so, it is apparent that 'materialism' is just another word for what we have termed 'realism'. Lenin needs a further argument to show that the real is in fact material. To do this we must give the word 'matter' some content. What precisely is it which is the only real thing? Lenin had to give a philosophic definition which would not be vulnerable to the investigations of physicists. He therefore says:[2]

> Matter, in the form of the limit which we have known up to now, vanishes, as our knowledge penetrates deeper: those properties of matter which before seemed absolute, immutable and primary (impenetrability, inertia, mass etc.) disappear, and now become relative, belonging only to certain states of matter. For the sole 'property' of matter — with the recognition of which realism is initially connected — is the property of being *objective reality*, of existing outside our cognition.

Lenin clearly believes that the objective reality of matter should not be confused with its manifestations, or even indeed with particular scientific theories about its structure. They may be superseded. Matter is a philosophic concept for him, and should be distinguished from the physical structure which is the concern of scientific investigation. In fact, Lenin's concept seems merely the expression of the ability of man to reflect on an external world. As such it seems no more than an assertion of realism. Lenin, however, thinks there are only two possible views in the theory of knowledge, and dubs these 'idealism' and 'materialism'. He conceives the former as being quite simply the doctrine that there is no object without a subject, and the latter that the object exists independently of the subject. He refuses to accept that there could be any kind of compromise position, and in fact thinks that any philosopher has to fit into one or other category. If a philosopher is not an uncompromising materialist, it follows, according to Lenin, that he is an idealist.

Even if we were to accept that the controversy between materialist and idealist is fundamental in the history of philosophy, it is unfortunately the case that Lenin is using the term 'materialism' in two different senses. The first is as a synonym for 'realism' where he is merely concerned to argue for the existence of objective reality, The second is a much more full-blooded one, and is in fact the usual sense. Lenin declares:[3]

> The materialist elimination of 'the dualism of mind and body'. . . consists in this, that the existence of the mind is shown to be dependent upon that of the body, in that mind is declared to be secondary, a function of the brain, or a reflection of the outer world.

Mind (or spirit) is thus merely an evolving aspect of matter which is primary. Lenin offers no further argument for this position. He assumes that it is entailed by the falsity of idealism, which makes mind primary and matter secondary. His own use of the word 'dualism' ought to have warned him that even within the terms he set himself, there is at least a third position, namely that mind and matter are of equal importance, and neither can be reduced to the other. However that may be, Lenin seems to ignore the fact that realism does not entail materialism. He attempts to show the falsity of idealism by arguing for realism, but he then thinks quite illegitimately that he has established materialism. It is only fair to point out that Lenin was aware of the term 'realism'. He says:[4]

We call attention to the fact that the term 'realism'is here employed in a sense contrary to idealism. Following Engels, I will use the term 'materialism' in this sense, accounting it as the only correct one, especially since the term 'realism' has been usurped by positivists and other muddle-heads who vacillate between materialism and idealism . . . Naive realism is the instinctive materialist viewpoint held by humanity which accepts the existence of the outer world independently of mind.

One of Lenin's main motives for attempting to establish the truth of materialism was his atheism. He associated idealism with 'clericalism' and concluded perfectly correctly that if he could only establish materialism, he would rule out any possibility of the existence of any non-material entity such as God. Once he had shown the existence of an objective world as the only origin of human experience, any view not grounded in our view of that objective reality would be demonstrably false. The source of truth resided in the material world, which is the sole reality. The world existed long before men did, whereas, 'if truth', he says[5] 'is an organizing form of human experience, then any assertion about the existence of the earth without the experience of men cannot be true'. If truth merely has its source in human experience, then, he asserts, 'a place is cleared to house the "organizing forms" of the religious experience'.

Once again, Lenin's arguments do not establish materialism, but only realism. It may be unsatisfactory to talk of truth as an 'organizing form of human experience'. It certainly seems to make truth depend on man, and spurns the notion of strong objectivity which Lenin seeks to defend. Yet his argument would work for God too. The existence of God cannot be made to depend on human experience, since, as Creator, He obviously existed before any men. The objective reality of God does not depend on man's conception of Him, which, however imperfectly, could perhaps be said to reflect that reality. Lenin needs the further premiss that objective reality is material, to block such an argument. He treats this, however, as his conclusion, rather than as something which has to be independently established.

Lenin's views are echoed in contemporary writing, with the same slide from realism into materialism. Those with a Marxist-Leninist philosophical background are, of course, unquestioning in their identification of matter and objective reality. For example, B. M. Kedrov[6], dealing at length with Lenin's views, notes approvingly that his philosophical concept of matter 'denotes the whole objective reality, without any limitations'. Yet even Western writers are often attracted by aspects of Lenin's conflation of the two. D-H. Ruben is fully aware of the significance of the terms 'materialism' and 'realism' and yet is quite content to run the two together, explicity following Lenin. Part of the trouble stems from the use of 'materialism' in contradistinction to 'idealism' to denote the existence of at least *some* non-mental things. Yet admitting that there are material objects, and claiming that all entities are material, are two very different positions. Ruben distinguishes[7] his view from that of a reductive materialist who claims that everything can be reduced to matter, but it then becomes unclear just why he calls himself a materialist, rather than a realist. He is obviously not very sure himself. He says, in emphasizing the independence of nature from the activity of man:[8] 'Marxian realism (or materialism—I henceforth use these interchange-ably) is the belief in an objective realm outside thought or mind *in the widest sense.*' Elsewhere we are told[9] that 'philosophical materialism asserts the real existence of things independently of the human mind'. Unless great weight is put on the word 'things', there is nothing in this definition of materialism to rule out the existence of the Christian God. Yet Ruben[10] also wants to claim that 'materialism is one form of atheism'. It is apparent that he does mean more by 'materialism' than simply 'realism'.

Antony Flew could certainly not be accused of writing with Marxist-Leninist assumptions, and he does not simply talk of realism and then think he has proved materialism. He combines Lenin's realism with arguments stemming from the later Wittgenstein on the importance for the existence of language of common access to public criteria for the uses of words. Flew writes:[11]

> The idea of the primacy of the material, which was involved in Lenin's further understanding of the great confrontation between idealism and materialism, can now be profitably enriched by including the notions of the semantic and epistemological priority of the public. . . It is a proposal carrying the illuminating consequence that both *The Concept of Mind* and the *Philosophical Investigations* have to be recognized as major contributions to the development of a modern materialism.

As Flew himself realizes, this is a highly controversial suggestion, although it is no doubt arguable, given apparently behaviourist tendencies to be found in those books. What is even more questionable, however, is whether the alleged materialism of Ryle and the later Wittgenstein has anything to do with Lenin's undoubted realism. In emphasizing the primacy of the public, Flew insists that a person's use of language must be publicly checkable. For example, memory claims which, as he says, could be backed by nothing more than an unverifiable or unfalsifiable conviction that a consistent usage was in fact being followed could not, he believes, count as knowledge. It then may seem reasonable to link what is publicly verifiable with what is material. This depends on the initial step of refusing to countenance what lies beyond verification or falsification, and this certainly cannot be called a realist position. Verificationist analyses typically limit what is to be accounted real to what is publicly accessible. We shall see how this has the result of making the existence of even parts of the physical world problematic, and it deals a fatal blow to the existence of anything non-material. Thus even if what is publicly accessible must be material, it does not follow that everything material must be publicly accessible, let alone that everything real must be. The materialism of those who insist that reality must be susceptible to public checks and tests is very different from that of Lenin. In so far as they limit reality to what is accessible to man, they are opponents of realism. By emphasizing Lenin's materialism, Flew has forgotten to give due weight to his realism. This merely serves to illustrate how different the two doctrines are. It is perfectly possible to assert one while denying the other.

The stress on the distinction between realism and idealism raises the large question of how theistic idealists conceive of God. Is the reality of God merely dependent on human minds or is it independent? The importing of God into an idealist system may seem attractive, since the dependence of material entities on an omniscient mind, instead of human ones, would certainly make them objective from our point of view. Ewing[12] states quite bluntly that 'the strongest type of idealism is theistic, for this type of idealism can alone secure objectivity'. A theistic idealism like this would from men's point of view indeed be largely indistinguishable from realism. The problem would be the status of God's reality, which, it appears, would be the source of all other non-mental reality (assuming that the independent reality of human minds is not being questioned). There is no point in securing the reality of the world by linking it to God, if His reality in turn merely depends on our judgements. On the other hand, we are forced into a realist position about His reality if He is independent of men's conceptions, and He would not seem worth worshipping if He were not. The dispute between realism and theistic idealism then becomes a dispute about *what* is independently real (for instance, whether material objects are). It is no longer about whether any part of reality can be independent of human thought. Indeed, as we have already pointed out, *any* non-solipsist idealism must involve epistemological realism. Anyone who is not a solipsist has to accept that there is *something* outside himself. The basic controversy between realists and their opponents is not so much about the relationship between reality and a particular individual as between reality and man in general. The distinction between weak and strong objectivity, between intersubjectivity and objectivity, is the crucial one.

One difficulty which faces any realist is the possibility of error. If we can be mistaken, how can we be sure that we are not always mistaken? Yet the very possibility of error appears to emphasize the existence of a reality beyond men's judgements in comparison with which they are sometimes found wanting. What is accepted as true today may be totally rejected for compelling reasons in a few years' time. This is particularly so in science, and is why Lenin made his concept of matter a regulative concept, so that his belief in materialism merely becomes a belief in a strongly objective world. The current state of scientific progress will dictate what we take to be objectively so. Lenin tried to balance his belief in objectivity with the fact of human fallibility. He fully accepted[13] that the state of knowledge at any given time represents only 'approximate reflections of an object which exists independent of humanity'. At the moment we only have partial truth. Thus Lenin can say[14] that the 'essence' of things is relative, as it 'expresses only the degree of man's power penetrating into and knowing objects'. He continues:

> Dialectic materialism insists on the temporary, relative approximate character of all the milestones on the road of knowledge of nature, through the progressive science of man. The electron is as inexhaustible as the atom, nature is infinite, but it *exists* infinitely: and only this categorical, unconditional recognition of its existence beyond the consciousness and sensation of man distinguishes dialectic materialism from relativist agnosticism and idealism.

The realist is in many ways in the same position as any opponent when he is forced to recognize that man's purported knowledge of the world is not fixed but develops. Lenin emphaiszes that it does develop towards a goal. Changes of belief are not merely random. It is clear though that excessive concentration on the development of belief and of the knowledge man thinks he possesses may encourage some to jettison any notion of the reality the beliefs are attempting to portray. The apparently dynamic character of knowledge can attract attention away from a reality which may appear static and irrelevant. Since, though, the very definition of knowledge entails that what is known is true, we shall see when we examine the sociology of knowledge that some are tempted to make reality itself dynamic. Instead of defining knowledge by reality, they define reality by knowledge. Lenin asserted[15] that 'all boundaries in nature are arbitrary, relative, moveable and express the gradual approximation of our reason toward the knowledge of matter'. One has only to reject the notion of matter, here portrayed, as involving an excursion into the inaccessible world of metaphysics, to be left with a notion of a nature in process in line with our changing beliefs. The shadow of Heraclitus, and his view that everything is in flux, certainly looms large. Lenin's insistence on the notion of matter existing independently of mind sometimes seems no more than an assertion of dogmatic faith belied by all the facts. The more inaccessible matter is, the more nature has to become the projection of our particular beliefs at a particular moment. In the field of science, Lenin seems content in fact, if not in theory, to relegate matter to the status of a reality hidden behind a succession of historically conditioned appearances. It is true that he held that we are always getting nearer absolute truth, but his approach to science is largely anthropocentric. His example should warn us that whatever fine words may be spoken about objective reality, it is still very easy to put it far beyond our reach. The result is that we have to concentrate on the ever-changing pattern of our beliefs and the reality-for-us described by them. It is not surprising that Marxist-Leninists emphasize the social character and determination of knowledge. Yet we must recognize his dilemma. It would be equally unacceptable to make objective reality what we happen to believe in here and now. The history of science should show us that even the most firmly held theories can one day be modified or even overthrown.

Anthropological Realism

This is not the place to begin any detailed exegesis of Karl Marx, but it is interesting to note the views developed by Leszek Kolakowski out of remarks made by Marx in the 1844 Manuscripts. They provide a good example of the kind of view which is basically anti-realist in that it does not pay any attention to objective reality independent of man. The early Marx himself said[16] that 'nature, taken in the abstract for itself, and fixed in its separation from man, is nothing for man'. Some interpretations conclude that he dismissed as devoid of sense anything like Lenin's notion of objective reality. Kolakowski elaborated a view which has been called[17] 'anthropological realism'. Yet it is very different from the kind of realism advocated by Lenin. We have here a further illustration of just how slippery a term 'realism' can be. For Kolakowski man is not a detached observer set apart from the world. He is a part of nature, and nature is the product of man. Whereas Lenin (and Engels) saw the development of men's concepts as an attempt to copy the external world more accurately, Kolakowski argues that they arise from the interaction between man and his environment. Man seeks to fulfil his needs, and shapes the world according to them. Nature is thus humanized nature, reality-for-us. Kolakowski says:[18]

> Human consciousness, the practical mind, although it does not produce existence, produces existence as composed of individuals divided into species and genera. . . It is this effort to subdue the chaos of reality that defines not only the history of mankind, but also the history of nature as an object of human needs —and we are capable of comprehending it only in this form.

Mankind and nature cannot be considered in isolation from each other, and we can only have access to a nature which already wears the 'imprint of the organizational power of man'.[19] The attributes of reality are 'socially subjective', rather than independent of man. They are divided up as they are because of man's practical needs. Kolakowski comments that as a result things in the world must be considered in some sense artificial. 'The sun and the stars exist' he says, 'because man is able to make them *his* objects.' He denies that any other division would be theoretically less justified or less 'true'. So far from language being a 'transparent glass' through whch one can contemplate the 'objective' wealth of reality, 'it is a set of tools we use to adapt ourselves to reality and to adapt it to our needs'.

Why should this position be called 'realist' even if it is an 'anthropological' realism? There is still a notion of reality, but the reality is only socially subjective. Common to all men, it can be distinguished from individuals. It is above all accessible, because it was created by man for man. Kolakowski draws[20] an analogy between this view of man and a notion of God, though not of God creating the world from nothing, but of God creating it out of previously existing material. Yet although reality is not independent of man, it is independent of particular judgements made by man. There is a sense, according to Kolakowski, in which the reality which is divided into species by language is born at the same time as the language. Thus he holds that his view maintains a classical definition of truth. True judgements would not correspond to the world 'in itself', but they would still correspond to that world upon which man has already imposed 'substantial forms'.

This only serves to stress that it is facile to link the correspondence theory of truth too closely with realism. It is all too easy to assume that any species of correspondence guarantees realism, and this is no doubt a reason why Kolakowski's view has attracted the 'realist' label. A measure of mutual independence is demanded for the two items where correspondence is supposed to contain the nature of truth. Kolakowski's espousal of Marxian 'naturalism' certainly involves contrasting the reality created by man (and in its turn affecting him) with the reality judged true by particular men at particular times. Yet Kolakowski makes the very nature of the only reality that matters (humanized reality) dependent on its relationship with man. As such, it must be judged anti-realist rather than realist.

In a picturesque phrase[21] Kolakowski concludes that in all the universe, 'man cannot find a well so deep that, leaning over it, he does not discover at the bottom his own face'. This sums up the anthropocentric nature of many philosophic theories. Not all of them would perhaps think of reality being created by man's needs in quite such a literal way, but all would link reality to man's understanding or to his language. Reality is for them restricted to what is accessible to men. It becomes 'reality-for-us' and we are told that it is meaningless to conceive of what cannot be expressed in language, or experienced.

Verification and Truth

We must distinguish between those who want to define truth by some notion of correspondence or agreement with reality, and those who turn instead to the idea of truth being related to what agrees with our experience. While even the former does not guarantee realism, the latter involves a radical departure from it. It may be suggested that reality must be experienced, if the notion of correspondence is to be meaningful. Correspondence with an ineffable and mysterious reality would be useless as a criterion for truth, and it may be thought that we cannot *mean* by 'true' a correspondence which we can never discover. Truth appears to be forever removed from our grasp unless reality can be experienced and expressed in language. The natural consequence is to insist that we mean by 'reality' empirical reality. In other words, reality is what we experience and hence we can talk about. This can be extended a little by importing counterfactuals and saying that reality is what we would experience if certain conditions were fulfilled. As we saw with Peirce, this claim can be weakened to the point that it is completely acceptable to a realist. It may be possible *in principle* for the truth of anything to be recognized by someone. If we start, as Peirce did, to envisage minds with different perceptual equipment and to allow an infinite time for recognition to take place, or if with Berkeley we import the omniscience of God into the system, then it follows that 'being' and 'being perceived' will coincide. Even then, there is room for argument between the realist and his opponents about whether existence depends on recognition, or whether the two are independent. There comes a point in all this, though, where the concept of empirical reality becomes emptied of all special meaning, and it becomes equivalent to mere reality. If the word 'empirical' is to have a particular force, it must restrict our ideas of what there is to what we humans may experience in a finite time.

The corollary of this is that truth becomes linked to the possibility of verification. The insistence that the truth or falsity of meaningful sentences must make a publicly observable or verifiable difference is the basis of the so-called 'verification principle'. It is held meaningless to talk of what is beyond such verification. Truth need not be reduced to the process of verification, since verificationists are usually content to allow for truth to be ascribed to situations where there has been no actual verification though it is possible. Nevertheless, although they may think truth is discovered by verification, it is clearly not logically independent of the possibility of verification. Since this is not an abstract thing, but verification by *men*, the theory is fundamentally anthropocentric. Truth is what men can find out. Usually it is what they can *in principle* find out, but truth is restricted by the limitations placed on men, if the process of verification is restricted to what is at present humanly possible. Verificationism may not make reality dependent on mind, but it does restrict truth to the possibility of experience. When it is assumed that reality is merely what is expressed by true propositions, the link between man and reality is as close as in any idealist system. In so far as reference is made to possible sense data or observations, the link between reality and mind is still there.

Verificationism is a theory about truth, but it does raise the question of the relationship of truth and reality. True propositions are about reality, and reality is described by true propositions. Both these statements sound innocuous. Indeed they may even be true by definition. (For the moment I am putting aside arguments about whether 'statement' or 'sentence' may be better than 'proposition' in this context.) It is not true that it is raining if it is not raining. The rain is correctly described by the proposition that it is raining. Yet even if we accept that what is true describes reality and that reality is described by what is true, are the two completely coextensive? The verificationists dismissed what was unverifiable as meaningless and nonsensical. This had the effect of denying the intelligibility of any reality beyond what men are equipped to talk about through observations. Michael Dummett argues[22] that if all the sentences of a language are decidable, it is possible for a theory of meaning for that language to be both 'realist and verificationist', since, 'explanation of sense in terms of truth conditions and in terms of verification coincide for such a language'. What is the case can then always be recognized as such. The verificationists were thus able to hold that something is either true or false, even though they refused to accept any separation between what was true and what could be recognized as true. They were only able to do this by restricting the notion of intelligibility. The verificationists' 'realism' consisted in ruling out the possibility of talking about what they could not recognize as true or false through sense-experience. It was a realism bought at the price of restricting reality to what men could accept as true. Like Peirce's dismissal of 'incognizables', the verificationist's use of the term 'meaningless' only serves to emphasize the anthropocentricity of the theory. Such a restriction on what could be real only makes the theory 'realist' by denying what lies at the heart of realism, that man's judgements must conform to reality rather than reality conforming to man's judgements.

Many, wishing to replace the notion of truth in a language with that of verification, would not accept that sentences are invariably either true or false. If they cannot be considered true or false independently of our knowledge, it follows that where we lack knowledge of their truth-values, we are not, in general, entitled to assume that they have them. The realist would wish to emphasize that they are true (or false), whether we find out or not, whereas truth without the possibility of its recognition would be a meaningless concept for the anti-realist. In fact his main preoccupation is very often with meaning. The precise relationship of meaning to truth in a language is a very large question, but it is obviously tempting to link the meaning of what we say to the conditions under which we recognize its truth. The realist, on the other hand, has to try and link meaning with the conditions under which a sentence *is* true. This will raise difficulties when it is impossible for us to decide what is true. If truth eludes our grasp, might not meaning do so as well? We may not be in a position to be sure of what we are asserting without the possibility of knowledge of what would make the sentence true or false. It seems that some accounts must be taken of human limitations.

Dummett says:[23] 'To describe what would make a state-ment true is to describe what it would be to recognize it as true, even if the means of recognition are not available to us.' As a gloss on this, he points out that even if this is interpreted in a way acceptable to the realist, it does impose certain limits on what ranges of statements can be given a re-alistic interpretation. There has, he believes, to be some analogy between 'the perceptual and mental operations which we perform and those hypothetical ones of which we are incapable but by tacit reference to which we acquire a grasp of the less primitive expressions of our language, according to the realist interpretation of our language'. What we can meaningfully say about reality, then, cannot be too far removed from the means we have available for recognizing when something is so or not. Even if as men we are unable to break through the physical limitations imposed on us, we have to be able to have some conception of what it would be like to do so and thus recognize the truth of what we are saying. There comes a point when we have to ask what content our claims about reality have, if they are totally cut asunder from any means we could envisage for finding out if they are accurate. Whether one wants to emphasize the link between meaning and truth-conditions or between meaning and verification, there must, it is argued, still be *some* link between meaning and the recognition of truth. The realist might thus, it seems, be forced to concede that talk of reality, though not of course reality itself, is limited by what it is possible for us to conceive. Conversely the constant pressure on the verificationist is to move away from reference to actual verification and switch to mere verification in principle.

The gap between the two might not appear so wide, but an important distinction remains. A realist would hold that a meaningful sentence is either true or false whether one can decide or not. Dummett calls this 'the fundamental tenet of realism'. An anti-realist talking of the possibility of verification may allow that some sentences are undecidable. They are neither true nor false, although they must be the kind of sentences the truth of which can be determined when the conditions are right. An anti-realist would hold that it is wrong to talk of truth or falsity when we have no means of verification. Such sentences may be intelligible, but not decidable. On this line of reasoning, which Dummett himself appears to favour, truth is linked to human capacity and to the evidence which is in fact available.

Dummett even envisages[24] one type of anti-realist applying his view to statements about the past, so that 'only those statements about the past are true whose assertion would be justified in the light of what is now the case'. A consequence of this, he thinks, is that there is no one past history of the world, but 'every possible history compatible with what is now the case stands on an equal footing'. The connection between truth and reality seems well and truly broken in this example. Truth is linked instead with what we are justified in asserting. Yet Dummett thinks that on this position it could be held that there is no *one* past history. We have to start from where we are, and truth is linked to present evidence. As a result, assertions about *reality* are based on present evidence. This may not itself seem particularly obnoxious. It expresses the truism that we are only justified in talking about what we are justified in talking about. The anti-realist's view is stronger than this, and does not just limit what we can say about reality, but it limits reality itself to what we can now say it is. Otherwise, it could accept that there has been one past even though we may not be able to say what it was like. Yet this whole way of putting the problem could be portrayed as a massive begging of the question. The implication that reality is in some mysterious way beyond language is precisely what is often denied by the anti-realist. Reality is what we are in a position to say it is, and does not exist in some misty way beyond our reach. We were wrong to say that Dummett is breaking the link between truth and reality. That might be so from a realist point of view, since truth is linked to the available evidence rather than to the way things are, regardless of our state of knowledge. Dummett's argument ensures that no meaning can be attached to the latter kind of reality. 'Reality' means accessible reality.

He defines[25] realism as the belief that 'for any statement there must be something in virtue of which either it or its negation were true'. All statements are either true or false whether or not they are decidable. Dummett accepts that a statement is true 'only if there is something in the world in virtue of which it is true'. He would part company from the realist in thinking that *all* statements are true or false, and would say that if we cannot decide the truth of a sentence for lack of evidence, there *is* nothing in the world in virtue of which it is true. 'The world' or 'reality' is the world as *we* see it or reality *for us*. After starting with the problem of meaning, he has ended up with making what are apparently ontological claims. Dummett believes that there can be something in virtue of which a statement is true or false only if the statement is of such a kind 'that we could in finite time bring ourselves into a position in which we were justified either in asserting or denying it'. What there is therefore depends on what we are in a position to recognize as obtaining. Claims about what exists are empty unless we have knowledge of a particular instance of what we are talking about. The anti-realist typically ties the truth of certain statements to the occurrence of particular conditions which we are taught to accept as justification of their assertion. Dummett says:[26] 'In the very nature of the case, we could not possibly have come to understand what it would be for the statement to be true independently of that which we have learned to treat as establishing its truth.' The truth conditions of a statement are thus tied to the kind of conditions in which we first learnt its meaning. The conditions under which we acquire concepts become the truth conditions of statements employing the concepts. They thus become the reality the concepts are intended to apply to. Under this view 'reality' can never be inaccessible, since it is normally no more than the circumstances under which we learnt the meaning of what we wish to say.

As John McDowell admits,[27] there is something right about saying: 'Only realism presupposes the reality of the past; anti-realism represents the past as unreal in itself, enjoying a sort of vicarious existence in its traces.' Needless to say, this is too simple, and McDowell points out that the argument is one over *how* the reality of the past is to be conceived. His formulation of the anti-realist's view (which he does not share) is that 'certain specific events and states of affairs occurred and obtained: a thought to which he is committed by past-tensed assertions which, according to his theory, present circumstances entitle him to make'. This sounds like the position of common sense, until it is realized that it maintains that the past consists only of the particular events which we are entitled to talk about because of our *present* circumstances. It thus becomes impossible to be ignorant of the inaccessible parts of the past, since, at least as far as we are concerned, they did not exist. *Ex hypothesi*, we have no evidence for them.

McDowell considers that the realist's view of the reality of the past can be described, 'with only the mildest caricature, as the idea of another place, in which past events are still occurring, watched, perhaps, by God'. This is, in fact, a *gross* caricature. The realist need never be involved in such metaphysical absurdities, merely because he insists that what happened once is logically independent of what we are now in a position to assert happened. What happened in the past happened in the past, and it is indeed for this simple reason that present evidence may not be good enough.

Analogous problems, about the relationship of evidence with what it is evidence for, arise with the question of the reality of 'other minds'. The anti-realist will always try to tie apparently mental events with public criteria, so as to link the meaning of our concepts with the conditions under which we learnt them and continue to apply them. McDowell, for instance, tries to tread a middle path between anti-realism and some forms of realism. He sketches[28] a position according to which, at least on the occasions suitable for teaching the relevant parts of language, 'one can literally perceive in another person's facial expression or his behaviour, that he is in pain, and not just infer that he is in pain from what one perceives'. The anti-realist is always concerned with the question how we can have a conception of, and use language meaningfully about, states of affairs of a kind inaccessible to us. McDowell puts it this way:[29] 'To say that God, or another person who is in pain, or a participant in a historical event, knows or knew, what is in question does nothing towards showing how it is possible that we do.' In this he is consciously echoing Dummett who insists[30] that we answer the question 'how we come to be able to assign to our sentences a meaning which is dependent on a use to which we are unable to put them'. Dummett feels it is hopeless to show how we grasp the truth conditions of sentences by, for example, appealing to beings with powers which we do not possess and imagining that they could decide the truth of these sentences.

Dummett says:

> Even the most thoroughgoing realist must grant that we could hardly be said to grasp what it is for a statement to be true if we had no conception whatever of how it might be known to be true; there would, in such a case, be no substance to our conception of its truth condition.

Linking reality with the possibility of knowledge is apparently innocuous. Once, however, one demands that the latter be defined by more than its link with reality, one is thereby putting constraints on it and hence on the notion of reality. For example, the possibility of knowledge can be limited by the abilities or spatio-temporal position of those obtaining it. Dummett's 'thorough-going realist' has given considerable hostages to fortune. He must soon concede that knowledge is impossible in certain areas, and he therefore loses grip on the notion of reality in them, or he must insist that knowledge is in principle possible, even if we have no conception of how this might be so. Since, however, he has already conceded that we cannot grasp what it is for a statement to be true in those circumstances, his 'realism' has become very suspect.

There are three separate stages, the truth of a statement, knowledge of the truth, and our conception of how that knowledge is possible. Linking the first with the second is risky for a realist, but linking it with the third as well is to restrict truth to what is within *our* ability to conceive. It is, no doubt, a major task to explain our understanding of sentences when their truth conditions are beyond our grasp. How can the meaning of a sentence far outstrip the kind of circumstances in which we first learnt it, and indeed the kind of circumstances to which we ever have access? Nevertheless the substance which our conception of truth conditions has cannot dictate what the truth conditions are, on a genuine realist view. Otherwise, they merely become a subtle form of verification conditions. Dummett's 'realist' has already given up the basic tenet of realism by allowing the notion of truth to be limited by our conceptions.

Realism demands that an adequate theory of meaning must recognize that inaccessible truth is not a contradiction in terms. Indeed, as Strawson points out, once meaning is related to verification conditions, a sentence in the mouths of those who do not have access to them, in fact or principle, has a different meaning from that in the mouths of those who do. He insists:[31] 'The conception of verification-transcendent truth-conditions . . . and its link with that of meaning is an essential part of a general view of the world which is in no way contrary to reason and to which we are in any case inescapably committed.'

Anti-realists in this context arrive at their position by considering the problem of meaning, rather than by directly juxtaposing mind and reality and asking which is prior. They are concerned with language as the expression of mind, and indeed sometimes seems to make linguistic capacity the defining feature of mind.[32] The emphasis in contemporary philosophy often seems to have shifted from the philosophy of mind to that of language, and this is no accident. Modern versions of the controversy between realists and idealists may, as a result, often be couched in terms of the relationship between *language* and reality. Is reality defined by what language is capable of expressing, or is it totally extra-linguistic, being itself what language tries to be about? The problem of the relation of concepts and reality itself straddles the distinction between mind and language. Concepts can be thought of as wholly mental, or as public and enshrined in language. If the latter, different languages may express different concepts and it is hardly surprising that the problem of translation looms large in the writings of philosophers of language. There is a problem of understanding other languages, when there is no guarantee that they employ similar concepts to our own.

The revolt against the notion of private concepts in the mind has been largely stimulated by Wittgenstein's famous arguments against the possibility of a private language. His view that meaning is use is a good example of an anti-realist position, where the meaning of an expression is tied to the way it is used, and the way it is used reflects the public conditions under which it was taught. Such an approach will inevitably restrict what can be counted as real to what is accessible. It has indeed to be *publicly* accessible, since Wittgenstein will have no truck with 'private objects' independent of any public criteria. Pains which are not unpleasant and thus not expressed in behaviour fall into this category. Anybody[33] who wishes to say that pains are defined by their quality, and need not always be disliked, will have to hold that they are independent of the public conditions under which the concept of pain is taught. In that case the circumstances in which a person is taught the concept will include the fact that they are feeling a sensation of a certain sort. It could be argued that this is more a question of whether what is verifiable must be publicly so, rather than a straight opposition between what is true and what can be recognized as such. How far should the recognition be public? Would my recognition that I have a pain be sufficient? Wittgenstein would of course say that it was not and that my claims must be susceptible to public checking. Otherwise there is always the possibility of an unintentional mistake which can never be uncovered. The emphasis on public criteria is, however, a natural development for any anti-realist view. Any step back from 'reality' to what is recognized as real is inevitably a step from strong objectivity to the notion of objectivity as intersubjective agreement.

What is public becomes all-important, if what is so is merely what is agreed to be so. Agreement between different individuals can only be obtained through access to criteria which are in principle available to all.

Wittgenstein often seems to be not so much challenging the reality of mental states such as pain, as saying that they are irrelevant to understanding the concept. This is a fairly common predicament. We cannot say anything about a reality beyond our reach and the temptation will always be to let the 'object' drop out of consideration as irrelevant.[34] What started as a 'bracketing off' of reality becomes a denial of its relevance, and then finally a denial of its existence. The term 'inconceivable' is a favourite of philosophers. It can mean what is beyond our comprehension because of the limitations placed on our understanding, but it can also be synonymous with 'logically impossible'. It is inconceivable that there be a round square since such a figure would be simultaneously both round and not round. Yet not everything which is inconceivable is logically impossible. Some things may simply go against what we think possible. Experts might find it inconceivable that a particular party could win an election against the odds. That does not mean it could not happen and, indeed, it sometimes does. Such a use of the term is not particularly interesting from a philosophical point of view. Other things lie beyond our capacity as humans to understand. Someone might, for instance, find the possibility of life after death inconceivable. It is here vital to sort out just what is meant. Are they saying it is logically impossible to survive death? Some philosophers certainly believe that the notion of such survival is as totally incoherent as that of a round square. Others, however, may merely mean that we have not at the moment the concepts adequate to characterize it. They may find it difficult even to say what 'it' is, and this is one of the problems, but it would be rash to conclude from this that there could be no such thing. Realities which cannot be characterized should not be dismissed as being in the category of the logically impossible. Yet if all our attention is directed on what is now accessible to man, such realities can all too easily be brushed aside. 'Objects' which drop out of consideration as irrelevant can soon lose any status as objects which they might still possess. It is perhaps no accident that Wittgenstein's preoccupation with the conditions necessary for the holding and transmission of concepts and his use of the particularly tricky example of sensations led him to be dubbed a behaviourist in some quarters. Behaviourism actually denies the reality of mental states and is thus a typical kind of anti-realist position. The slide from the dismissal of any reality but 'reality-for-us' as irrelevant down to its complete denial is a comfortable and natural one.

Realism and Language

Anti-realism can surface in many different contexts and forms as our reference to behaviourism illustrates. It is fact an all-pervasive philosophic attitude. The insistence that we cannot refer to entities which lie beyond our capability of recognizing in a finite time appears in many areas. There is nothing to prevent someone adopting an anti-realist position in certain contexts and not in others. One may indeed adopt an anti-realist stance concerning other minds and tend to behaviourism precisely because one wishes to be a realist concerning the objects open to scientific investigation. There are many 'scientific realists' who would want to dismiss anything outside the scope of contemporary science in general, and physics in particular. They would nevertheless stress the independent reality of physical entities. Anti-realism has typically to be served with at least a dash of realism.

Dummett introduced anti-realism by comparing it with intuitionism in mathematics. Classical mathematics accepts that every proposition is either true or false whether it can be proved or not. Intuitionists reject truth in favour of provability, and it must be borne in mind that there is no reason to assume that every mathematical proposition can, even in principle, be proved or disproved. Dummett thinks that this involves denying the Law of the Excluded Middle (every proposition is either true or false), but it might be better to say that the intuitionists have reinterpreted that law. They do not explicitly deny it, because they have no use for 'truth' or 'falsity'. The meanings of the logical connectives are to be understood in terms of provability.[35] The connectives stay the same but have a different meaning. The theories of classical propositional calculus can remain for intuitionist propositional calculus. For instance p simply means 'p is provable'.

This points to a problem concerning the understanding of truth. I have already noted that the correspondence theory of truth can be retained even when the notion of reality has been radically altered, so that it is no longer self-subsistent. Dummett can accept the view that there must be something in the world in virtue of which any true statement is true, while adding the proviso that it must be epistemically accessible. What appears a characteristically realist insight becomes acceptable to an anti-realist, if the terms involved are re-interpreted. Truth can be defined as the agreement, or correspondence, of judgements with how things are. This may appear a full-blooded realist position and is often accepted as such. Certainly it is when it is assumed that reality is not dependent on anything else for its existence. In the case of the physical sciences this means that the reality they investigate would be independent of man. We must be careful, though, about making independence of man the definition of reality, since it rules out man himself as having no share in reality. It also makes it impossible, by definition, for psychology or anthropology, for example, to be realist in any way, because they purport to be sciences about man. Their objects of study could not exist independently of men, because they will *be* men. A term such as 'self-subsistence' indicates that in these contexts the object of investigation is independent of the judgements made about it by psychologists or anthropologists.

Once 'how things are' is limited to what we are in a finite time able to recognize, the suggested definition of truth can still be accepted, but it is no longer a realist one. When the switch is made from 'reality' to 'reality-for-us' we turn from realism to anti-realism. It has often been the ambition of philosophers to reduce talk of physical objects to talk about phenomena. True statements would be about physical objects, but since the latter were equivalent to phenomena, truth would in fact correspond to things as they appeared to us. Realism and idealism would converge if that programme could be carried out, and this conflict would be seen as a completely bogus one. Truth, however, could still accepted as correspondence.

The conception of truth taken by many philosophers to be the only possible one is Tarski's, according to which a predicate, F, will be a truth predicate for a language only if it satisfies every instance of the schema ' "p" is F if and only if p', where 'p' is some sentence of the language in question. Thus it is essential to what we mean by 'true' that we are able to say, for example, that 'snow is white' is true if and only if snow is white. The point is that truth is made a predicate of sentences, and that a sentence is named in the first part of the definition and asserted in the second part. The whole thing has less of the air of the blindingly obvious and trivial if one names a sentence of a different language from the one the definition is given in. For instance, 'Il pleut' is true if and only if it is raining. The general policy is that to understand ' "p" is true', take 'p' out of quotation marks. Thus ' "it is raining" is true' means it is raining. This is not the place to investigate the reasons underlying this approach or its subtle ramifications. We are merely concerned with whether it is realist or not. The answer must be that it depends on the interpretation put on the words used. The second half of the definition involves an assertion. For instance, we may say that snow is white. An idealist is not constrained by his philosophical position from making remarks about snow. He just believes that physical objects are constructions out of the way they appear to us. For him 'snow is white' does not refer to something 'out there', but rather to our sense-impressions. He would use the words in the same situation as a realist and yet he would differ in his estimate of it. He would not think when he was looking at snow that he was confronted by something existing apart from it being perceived. Of course, it may be something of a miracle that everybody happens to have similar sense-impressions on similar occasions even though they have no common origin. That is not our present concern. The point is that even Berkeley would have agreed that 'snow is white' is true if and only if snow is white.

The same holds for a verificationist or any form of anti-realist. Unverifiable statements can be ruled out as meaningless and Tarski's definition can still hold. No meaningless statement could be true, and the statements which were still held to be true could still be slotted into Tarski's criterion of adequacy. A verificationist would be happy about 'snow is white' but perhaps not about 'God is omnipotent'. According to Tarski, 'God is omnipotent' is true if and only if God is omnipotent. Yet a verificationist would not wish to say that God was omnipotent. He probably would not want to talk of God at all, so the statement (or purported statement) could never even be for him a candidate for truth. However controversial his view may be, arguments would not arise over what he meant by 'true'. He can agree about that and still argue about which statements are genuine. The dispute would ultimately be about what kind of things could be meaningfully talked about, and this in turn becomes a question about what can be counted real. The verificationist does not have a different doctrine of truth; he rules out of court unobservable entities.

If what exists is self-subsistent, it does not depend on observation or other forms of recognition for it to be what it is. It follows that it could exist without anyone knowing. This is the thrust of the realist argument and it is denied by anti-realist. It is a dispute about what can be said to exist, or, as the realist might want to add, about what might exist even when we are not in a position to say anything about it. We are confronted with a question of metaphysics rather than an argument about a definition. We have to decide what can be allowed as real before we can know in virtue of what our statements are true. Tarski's criterion is philosophically neutral. Perhaps this is not surprising, since it might be very odd if what we meant by truth depended wholly on what we were willing to accept as true. No-one would then be able to disagree about what was true, since, if they did, that would show they meant something different by 'truth'. Major philosophical disagreements have not only occurred over the meaning of truth, but also over what kinds of entity true statements could be about.

Truth is a semantic category, not a metaphysical one. Restrictions on meaning, and hence on what can be true in a language, can have metaphysical implications. A verification theory of meaning dismisses all metaphysics as nonsense because it is not verifiable according to current scientific criteria. In the end, however, considerations of what can be meaningfully said and truthfully said necessarily involve concentration on what can be said. The adequacy of language in describing reality, and the status of reality apart from or sometimes even beyond language, cannot be linguistic questions. Even the adoption of an anti-realist stance which would justify concentraction on language is not itself a linguistic matter. There is a very real sense in which undue preoccupation with language involves a modern form of idealism. Philosophers are in effect saying that nothing exists unless it can be expressed in language. Reality becomes reality as portrayed by language. When 'mind' becomes 'linguistic capacity', the parallel with the idealism of former days becomes even more marked.

It may seem unwise to push any comparison too far between traditional idealism and the 'anti-realism' arising from the philosophy of language. The self-subsistence of the world, as described by language, need not be explicitly denied by the anti-realist. He has merely to refuse to accept the possibility that 'the world' can be understood as anything other than what is expressible in language. Nevertheless, although he may still think of language being *about* the world, language determines for him what the world is. What lies beyond the reach of language cannot be referred to, and is hence totally ruled out. The position, with all its ambivalence, is well summarized by the following remark:[36]

> 'Anti-realism is not a species of idealism. We do not ordinarily think of those aspects of reality which we are able conclusively to determine as any less *of* the world. All that is being suggested here is that such aspects constitute the world—or, at least, those of its features to which we can give intelligible expression.'

The world, it seems, may be objective, but its limits are set by language. 'Reality' is still only 'reality-for-us'. The full implications of this are made somewhat vague by the writer. It is controversial to say that we can only intelligibly talk about what can be conclusively determined. This is to limit the scope of language. It is more startling to say that 'the world' is constituted by what can be conclusively determined. This is a metaphysical thesis, restricting reality to what is accessible. His hesitation between the two, with the implication that they are not very different, is very significant.

The restriction of reality to what can be intelligibly talked about has the consequence that any conclusion about the limitations on language puts restrictions on the nature of reality. Anti-realists must indicate in what sense features of the world are logically prior to language, if they want to dissociate themselves from idealists. They seem to make the different parts of the world dependent on language, not only to be intelligibly talked about, but to be accepted as real. Furthermore, they make no distinction between what is accepted as real in language and what *is* real. Realists in the philosophy of language must not be content just to stress the impossibility of reducing truth conditions to verification conditions. They must also be prepared to accept that what is inexpressible in language could still be real. It is a mistake to think that the argument with the anti-realist is merely one about meaning and truth within language. It should also be about the limitations of language itself. Any concentration on the distinctions made *within* language between the real and the unreal is bound to be beside the point. The realist should insist on a reality *beyond* what language expresses. If something is impossible, this may be the result of a deficiency in our language. The limits of our language could be the limits of *our* world, but they are not the limits of *the* world. Pretending that they are is to insist on anthropocentricity.

Even Putnam, who is sympathetic to some form of realism, narrows the scope of the argument between the realist and anti-realist. He refers[37] to realism as the belief in a 'Describable world of unobservable things', confronting a view of 'unobservable things' as mere theoretical conveniences. The dispute about the status of unobservable entities is an important one in present-day physics, but it is not the only possible kind of dispute between a realist and his opponents. The realist may not just be concerned with what is unobservable but describable. He could also hold a belief in a world of unobservables which is *indescribable*. Needless to say, he should not be expected to say anything about such a world, but on realist principles there seems to be nothing against asserting its existence, as long as the indescribability did not stem from any logical incoherence. It is surely possible to raise a doubt about the limitations of language, particularly human language, since the latter is obviously closely bound up with the limitations, physical and otherwise, placed on man.

The realist belief in strong objectivity, with its consequent insistence that many things are beyond the powers of our language or our understanding to grasp, raises serious problems. We cannot talk of what is inexpressible, so we are not even in a position to say that we cannot put 'it' into words. What is 'it'? One response is to point to what happens in science as scientific knowledge grows and its vocabulary continually increases. New words have to be produced to refer to new entities as they are discovered. The realist view of science is that the categories used by scientists are intended to reflect real distinctions in nature. Without this simple belief, it becomes totally mysterious what scientists are attempting to do. The success of science is even more puzzling. It may be illusory. We may be merely imposing a conceptual system quite arbitrarily on the world around us. In that case, though, what is 'the world'? Is nature merely a projection from ourselves? Any belief that science is genuinely progressing, with scientists steadily acquiring new knowledge, is inexplicable without the realist view.

Realism is compatible with the view that human understanding and language are not static. In fact, it positively demands that we accept this, since it gives an explanation for changes which would otherwise seem arbitrary. *Why* should we change our view of the world unless our knowledge is increasing? The objection may be raised that intersubjective agreement, perhaps based on a similarity in sense impressions, can provide a firm enough basis in science. Yet it is a puzzle why the sense impressions should be similar unless there is an external world. Nevertheless, we must now consider the merits of intersubjectivity rather than strong objectivity. Although, as we have seen, realism can be applied differently in different contexts, we shall be looking primarily at science, since this provides a test case for realism. It is hardly likely to be successful in any other area if the world investigated by scientists is not self-subsistent. The material world has always been most resistant to an idealist interpretation.

There is a tendency in some quarters to restrict the possibility of knowledge to the sphere of science, so that what cannot be known as the result of scientific procedures cannot be known. 'Scientific realism' is a term that can be bandied around in a rather belligerent tone. Putnam[38] comments that it is 'reminiscent of nineteenth century materialism or, to be blunt about it, village atheism'. If the concern of science is thought to be exclusively *physical* reality, the restriction of realism to the domain of science involves a metaphysical decision about what there is. Even the resolve to stick to physics and eschew metaphysics is itself a metaphysical one. Our present preoccupation with science should not be taken to imply any such arbitrary judgement. What there is certainly includes the objects of science. Whether it only consists of them is a further problem. Many philosophers could produce other candidates to which they would want to attribute existence, whether they are the traditional ones such as God, minds, or souls, or abstract entities such as numbers, propositions, or even 'possible worlds'.

3 SCIENCE, REALISM AND QUINE

Realism in Science

'Truth' can be interpreted in different ways. Philosophers can agree which sentences are true while disagreeing about what makes them true. Insisting that certain scientific theories are true does not go to the heart of the dispute between the realist and his opponents. Realism has to provide an interpretation of truth whereby if a theory is true, then there are in the world the entities which the theory says there are. Even the insistence that all scientific theories are true or false, whether we can recognize their truth and falsity or not, is realist precisely because of the assumption that 'the world' gives theories their truth-value. Truth does not depend on our own abilities. We may, with Tarski, regard truth as a property of sentences, but language does not produce truth. Sentences in a scientific theory do not obtain their truth in virtue of their relation with other sentences. Although a theory can only be stated in a language, and although truth is always truth in a particular language according to Tarski, this need not involve linguistic relativity. What makes the sentences of a particular language true is the reality lying beyond language. The realist has to insist that the relationship of world to object is more fundamental than any relationship of word to word.

One consequence of the realist position in science concerns the status of theories and observations. The latter provide a crucial contact with external reality, and are the very cornerstone of science for the empiricist. He would hold that theories have to be 'cashed out' in terms of sensory experience, and are merely ways of organizing sensory data and producing predictions of future data. Scientific theories are in this way built on a firm foundation, provided by our experience of reality rather than reality itself. Empirical reality is always reality as experienced by men, and empiricists leave no room for any reality beyond experience. As we shall see, this becomes particularly crucial in fields such as quantum mechanics where physicists deal with purported entities which seem in principle to lie beyond experience. Empiricists hold that what cannot be observed or measured cannot be real. Observability provides the standard which theories have to meet. They have to explain past and present observations and to predict future ones.

There has been much debate in recent years about whether observation terms can in fact be 'theory-neutral'. May not the particular theory one holds determine what counts as an observation? The argument has concerned the very foundation of empiricism. The great danger of such an approach is that one's grip on reality is completely broken, and there seems no way of rationally deciding between theories, if reality can never be experienced as it is. The virtue of the empiricist emphasis on observations is that at least an independent test was available for theories. Theories do not seem to be *about* anything if reality is no more than what they posit. It becomes so dependent on theory that there is no possibility left of a theory ever being mistaken about an entity. The theory does not refer to entities which are self-subsistent and as a result cannot give a mistaken description of reality. When it is changed, it does not make a different assessment of the same things. It—or rather the new theory replacing the old one—merely picks out new entities. The history of science is thus pictured as involving a continuing series of discontinuities. Jumps are made from one theory to the next and the world posited by each successive theory is a different world. T. Kuhn has popularized this position more than anyone else. He has been influenced by the work of Quine, and summarizes his own position as follows:[1]

Proponents of differents theories (or different paradigms, in the broader sense of the term) speak different languages—languages expressing different cognitive commitments, suitable for different worlds. Their abilities to grasp each other's viewpoints are therefore inevitably limited by the imperfections of the processes of translation and of reference determination.

Some of the holders of this kind of view advocate an 'epistemological anarchism' which seems to result in complete nihilism. For instance, Paul Feyerabend advocates a 'pluralistic methodology' in science. He says:[2]

> Knowledge so conceived is not a series of self-consistent theories that converges towards an ideal view; it is not a gradual approach to the truth. It is rather an ever-increasing *ocean of mutually incompatible (and perhaps even incommensurable) alternatives,* each single story, each fairy tale, each myth that is part of the collection forcing the others into greater articulation.

A view like this could regard competition as merely a good method of arriving at truth. Feyerabend comments[3] that 'given any aim, even the most narrowly 'scientific' one, the non-method of the anarchist has a greater chance of succeeding than any well-defined set of standards, rules, prescriptions'. A rigid scientific method might not seem to be as good at producing results as a more anarchic approach. This might be argued from the history of science with *some* plausibility, but it is easy to pass from the view that the more views there are the better the chance of arriving at truth, to the belief that it does not matter what one believes because each view is as good, or bad, as any other. The first view is bound to develop into the second, without the notion of extra-theoretical reality. It is no accident that Feyerabend can talk of 'fairy tales'. The most sophisticated scientific theory has no more authority for him than the simplest fairy tale. He explicitly says: 'science has no greater authority than any other form of life'. This might just mean that it has no monopoly over truth. Scientific method does not provide the only access to reality. Feyerabend, however, means that *nothing* has access to reality, and that science is mere ideology. He is helped to this nihilistic position by his notion of what 'the world' is. He says:[4] 'There is only one task that we can legitimately demand of a theory, and it is that it should give us a correct account of the world, i.e. of the totality of facts *as constituted by its own basic concepts.*'

Thus incommensurable theories can each give a correct account of 'the world', merely because 'the world' is going to be defined differently in different theories.

Feyerabend has been called[5] a realist, albeit a radical and 'contemporarily fashionable' one. He is certainly no empiricist, and realists may agree with him about the priority of theories over observations. They will, though, be properly sceptical about his contempt for observations as a source of knowledge of a world beyond men's theory. It is in fact difficult to see how he could be classified as any kind of realist, since he has lost all grip on any notion of external reality. His emphasis on the importance of theories, and on their incommensurability, makes reality totally dependent on man's judgements, and 'it' changes as our theories change. Feyerabend makes theory, rather than mind, the arbiter of reality, but his conception of the status of physical reality is not so very different from that of the idealist.

At this point, we will be faced with the old chestnut which is always produced. I have already considered it. This time it will be put in terms of theory and reality, rather than in terms of concepts or of minds. How can we have independent access to reality, and if we cannot, how can we avoid seeing reality in terms of theory? The persistent temptation for the realist is to make reality hidden and inaccessible behind our conceptions and theoretical descriptions. We may not always be successful in our theorizing, and the history of science is the history of continual revisions in pursuit of the goal. What is the goal? Scientists wish to give an *accurate* theoretical description of reality. It is an open question how much of reality is in fact open to scientific investigation, but scientists must aim at a true characterization of the world. Some theories may already be true, others may have to be modified, and still others may have to be given up completely. One of the ironies of epistemology is that we are not often in a position to know which is which. We may persistently hold on to a theory later shown to be worthless, or we might be tempted by apparent counter-evidence to give up a substantially true one.

This predicament is merely an illustration of the fact that we can know without knowing that we know. Every examination and every television quiz show proves this. We can answer a question hesitantly and think we are guessing. Yet if we give the right answer, and had once learnt it, it may be more reasonable to assume that we lack confidence rather than knowledge. Someone who says '1558 to 1603' very hesitantly, when asked for the dates of the reign of Elizabeth I is hardly likely to be guessing. He knows the right answer without knowing that it is the answer. He possesses knowledge and does not realize that what he possesses *is* knowledge. Knowledge can go hand in hand with doubt. It does not imply certainty any more than certainty entails being right. The history of the world is littered with people who were certain and wrong. The same predicament faces us in science. Our theories may in fact reflect reality to a greater or lesser extent, even though we do not know how far they do. Science's aim is to progress from our present position of presumably piecemeal knowledge to the situation where our whole conceptual scheme adequately mirrors reality. The entities posited by our theories would then be entities which actually exist. We would describe them and their interrelationships as they actually are. Even in that final state we may not know that we possess complete knowledge. Uncertainty about reality does not show that reality is inaccessible.

The reality investigated by science exists independently of

theory, but it is wrong to think on that account that it hides behind a veil, forever mysterious and ineffable. We must emphasize its self-subsistence while insisting that we can say true things about it. The physical world is what true scientific theories say it is. The task of scientists is to try to obtain a conceptual scheme which would correspond to the nature of physical reality. The reality which a true scientific theory is about is ontologically distinct from the theory. It must be strongly objective. Yet it seems to be 'merely' posited by the theory. What check can there be on theories to ensure that they are more than just socially conditioned projections from the minds of scientists? The empiricist insistence on observations was misguided in so far as it made observations the only basis for theory. It entails that we can have no theories about what is unobservable. The realist is prepared to widen the scope of theories beyond what is currently observable. Instead of building theories up from what we can now observe, he expects his theories to refer to entities which might be observed one day with different, and more sophisticated equipment. He can point to what might in principle be observed. Indeed a realist may not be very worried if he has to admit that only beings with different sentient powers from ourselves or in a very different position in the universe from ourselves would be able to make some of the observations.

The view that theory is prior to observations was favoured by Einstein. He is quoted[6] by Heisenberg as saying 'It is always the theory which decides what can be observed.' This might sound like Feyerabend's insistence on the theory-relative nature of observations, but it is important to distinguish the two positions. Einstein was talking in the context of research into the nature of sub-atomic entities, where observations are in principle limited. He was asserting the right of theory to outstrip observations and to talk of unobservable as well as of observable entities. Theories are not to be interpreted merely in terms of actual or possible observations, but can themselves be used to interpret observation statements. As Feyerabend says[7] with approval, 'a realist wants to give a unified account both of observable and of unobservable matters'. This is true whether or not theories are incommensurable, and whether or not there can be a neutral observation language.

The realist in science does not merely oppose the empiricist's view about the pivotal role of observations. He also emphasizes that science is *about* something and that theories attempt to capture reality as it is. It follows that only one completely correct account of the world is forthcoming. Different, competing theories will each view the world differently, but the realist will not be as content with that situation as Feyerabend seems to be and will want to ask which is the *right* one. He will not undervalue the role of observations in trying to answer this, since they provide him with his major point of access to reality. Theory may outstrip observation, but it cannot persistently ignore it. The positing of unobservables may be anathema to many empiricists, but it may make perfectly good sense to the realist, particularly when it is borne in mind that what is unobservable today may become observable with the introduction of more advanced technology.

There are many reasons why something might be unobservable. The realist in science will only be concerned if observation is logically impossible. In that case, it is clear that he is supposing the existence of a logically impossible entity and has a self-contradictory notion. He will not be afraid of the mere physical impossibility of observing something. Of course, part of his argument with the empiricist is over what constitutes logical as opposed to physical impossibility. He is worried far less than his opponents by the impossibility of verification. Here, as elsewhere, a generous interpretation of 'in principle' can bring the empiricist who talks of verification in principle near to an optimistic realist who thinks that if an entity exists, someone somewhere should have access to it somehow.

Quine's View of Scientific Theory

If we wish to allow for reference to unobservable entities, we must emphasize theory more than observation, while still trying to keep contact with the external world through sensory stimulation of a simple or sophisticated kind. W. V. Quine puts forward a view like this and seems to be a realist. His views are widely discussed by contemporary philosophers, and it is worth asking how adequate they are from a realist standpoint. He believes that all theories are empirically underdetermined. All men will receive similar sensory stimulation in similar circumstances and this can provide a basis for translation between different languages. Nevertheless there is always more than one theory which could rest on the same empirical base. A physical theory could be totally different from ours, posit completely different kinds of objects, and yet be empirically equivalent. One example Quine has given of how we devise theories to fit our observations is when we see a procession of three lumps moving along the surface of the water. Is there one Loch Ness monster, or, say, a school of dolphins? Obviously we might in this instance be able to make further observations, but there will be cases where empirical evidence never goes far enough. Quine would say this was true even at the level of the most fundamental and general physical theory. Although he approves of the maxim 'Don't venture farther from sensory evidence that you have to', he stresses the following:[8]

> What wants recognizing is that a physical theory of radically different form from ours, with nothing even recognizably similar to our quantification or objective reference, might still be empirically equivalent to ours, in the sense of predicting the same episodes of sensory bombardment on the strength of the same past episodes.

He comments that for this reason the 'scientific achievement of our culture becomes in a way more impressive than ever'. This is because it has managed to restrict our vision to a manageable range of alternatives, instead of losing us in a sea of competing possibilities. He comments, though, that this very achievement 'has fostered the illusion of there being only one solution to the riddle of the universe'.

Although influenced by Peirce's pragmatism, Quine criticizes his conception of there being one ideal terminus for scientific theory. There is no unique theory even in principle accessible. He says:[9]

> We have no reason to suppose that man's surface irritations even unto eternity admit of any one systematization that is scientifically better or simpler than all possible others . . . Scientific method is the way to truth, but it affords even in principle no unique definition of truth.

The information given by our senses is the bedrock of scientific theory, but Quine thinks that it is inconclusive and always will be. This view appears to challenge the common idealist belief that even if the world is a construction out of our experiences, we all build the same world. The result is that we can no longer take mutual understanding for granted, and it is no doubt for this reason that the problem of translation looms so large in Quine's work. A certain measure of intersubjective contact is guaranteed by the similarity of sensory stimulation. This provides the basis both for language learning and for the building of scientific theory. Quine refers[10] to 'intersubjective observability of the relevant circumstances at the time of utterance' and continues: 'It is this . . . that enables the child to learn when to assent to the observation sentence. And it is this also . . . that qualifies observation sentences as check points for scientific theory. Observation sentences state the evidence, to which all witnesses must accede.'

The public accessibility of the circumstances under which observation sentences are uttered can thus both ensure that we can learn the same language and that scientific theory can have a firm base. Solipsism can be ruled out. The aspect of Quine's position which most concerns us is his purported realism. Does he put forward a full-blooded realist position, and, if not, what more is needed, or, rather, what more is it possible to have?

Quine's willingness to depart from the empirical base of theory and language, and to assert the existence of unobservables indicates what could be a realist position. He certainly believes in the priority of theory over observation. The key question will be, as in the case of Feyerabend, whether he can allow for the self-subsistence of reality. Quine himself certainly considers that his readiness to go beyond the empirical evidence shows that he is no idealist. He would maintain that even if two theories were empirically equivalent, they could still be very different. There would be no possibility of pointing to anything to show that one theory was true and the other not. The only evidence available would *ex hypothesi* be equally in favour of either. The choice between them could only be made on criteria which have nothing directly to do with reality, such as the simplicity of the theory or our familiarity with what it posits.

Quine emphasizes that judgements of truth come *after* the adoption of a theory. This could lay him open to the charge that, like Feyerabend, he is making truth relative to theory, but this is not the case. Quine's views are not the expression of any ordinary kind of relativism, so much as the reflection of the persistent problem of the relation of concepts to reality. Judgements can only be made from within a conceptual scheme and are thus the expression of that scheme. Quine has been much influenced by Peirce, and the latter's injunction to set out from where we are is implicit in much of Quine's work. As a result, there can be no talk of 'reality' except through the conceptual scheme we hold. In this respect, Quine's basic position has some similarity to that of Rescher. There is a real world, but it has to be described in terms of our conceptual scheme. Quine would not talk of 'things-in-themselves' or want any philosophic inter-

pretation of scientific statements. He thinks that present
scientific theory should be taken at face value. What there is
then becomes what our present theories say there is. This can
easily appear to be a dogmatism about what we happen to
believe at any given time, and it does not take seriously
enough the feeling that even though we believe we are right
in what we say, we may be wrong.

Quine states his views challengingly in a well-known, and
even notorious, passage. He says:[11]

> As an empiricist, I continue to think of the conceptual
> scheme of science as a tool, ultimately, for predicting
> future experience in the light of past experience.
> Physical objects are conceptually imported into the
> situation as convenient intermediaries—not by defi-
> nition in terms of experience, but simply as irreducible
> posits comparable, epistemologically to the gods of
> Homer. For my part I do, *qua* lay physicist, believe in
> physical objects and not in Homer's gods; and I
> consider it a scientific error to believe otherwise. But in
> point of epistemological footing the physical objects
> and the gods differ only in degree and not in kind.

This might make it look as if Quine is saying that physical
objects no more exist than the Homeric gods and that they
are merely reflections of a particular scheme. The only
distinction would be that we believe in physical objects and
not in Homeric gods. Quine does not think that this makes all
the difference and points out that unlike physical objects,
Homeric gods are useless for the purpose of scientific
prediction. Yet he would deny that he is patronizing
something by calling it a posit. He says:[12]

> Everything to which we concede existence is a posit
> from the standpoint of a description of the theory-
> building process, and simultaneously real from the
> standpoint of the theory that is being built. Nor let us
> look down on the standpoint of the theory as make-
> believe: for we can never do better than occupy the

standpoint of some theory or other, the best we can muster at the time.

Quine would therefore refuse to accept that there is any distinction between posits and reality. Posits can be real, and indeed in positing certain entities we are saying they are real. The reason we would deny reality to Homeric gods is not that they are posits, but that they are not *our* posits. According to Quine, reality is, in effect, what we believe exists. In terms of our present conceptual scheme, he thinks that this means looking to scientists to tell us what reality is like. Indeed, epistemology is secondary to science for him and is 'only science self-applied'.[13] Its task is merely to ask how we know what we do know from science. His theory rules out the possibility of scepticism except as something parasitic on knowledge.

We only have access to reality through theory. All objects are the product of theory, in the sense that they are posited by a particular theory. Because we always speak from the standpoint of some theory or other, the question of the relations of the terms of one theory to those of another provides an important problem for Quine. The underdetermination of theory by empirical evidence means that any appeal to experience will not be sufficient to pin down the relevant terms. He is able to use this point to good effect when he deals with the theoretical entities of physics. He thinks that even our common-sense views about the world go beyond available data and that this would be so even if we included all past, present and future sensory data. He is thus able to conclude[14] that the fact that empirical evidence is not sufficient in physics to determine molecular behaviour is not surprising and is analogous to the basic indeterminacy which infests all theory. He says: 'Considered relative to our surface irritations, which exhaust our clues to an external world, the molecules and their extraordinary ilk are thus much on a par with the most ordinary physical object.'

He is, it seems, prepared to adopt as strong a realist stance about such theoretical entities as about ordinary physical objects. Such a position could be taken as a very tough realist one. Yet all it shows is that *if* Quine is a realist, he is prepared to apply his realism consistently to ordinary things and to whatever is posited by any branch of science. If his realism is questioned, it has to be questioned with regard to *everything*.

Quine's Predicament

Quine takes the priority of theories seriously. Reference to objects is dependent on theory. Since he denies the possibility of independent access to reality, we cannot say what there is without speaking from some theory or other. It follows[15] that 'it makes no sense to say what the objects of a theory are, beyond saying how to interpret or reinterpret that theory in another'. Different theories can identify different objects. Since we cannot get outside all theories to confront reality, our only task is to map the connections between different theories by attempting to translate between them. A theory is merely a body of sentences for Quine, and so this is a linguistic matter. It is exceedingly significant that Quine holds that the word – word relationship is more fundamental than the word – object one. Since reality must be reality-as-seen-by-a-theory, we cannot just look at reality and see what someone is talking about. There is always an inherent indeterminacy, so that there will not be an exact match between terms of different theories. They have to be related, sometimes with difficulty, through the medium of what Quine calls 'some chosen manuals of translation'.

The same kinds of problems occur in ordinary translation between different languages. Quine thinks that a certain indeterminacy is inevitable. There are occasions when different translations would appear equally satisfactory and there is even in principle no way of deciding between them. Quine's examples have been much discussed, but the point of interest for us is that he says[16] that 'there is no fact of the matter' in these instances of what he calls 'the inscrutability of reference'. Holding that there is would imply that we can get outside all languages and compare them with reality. Yet reality is seen *through* language, and different languages are underdetermined by the sensory experience which Quine considers gives us an intersubjective base as a common starting point. He is still enough of an empiricist to think that our common experience alone can fully justify a theory or provide a firm basis for language. His use of the term 'indeterminacy' itself involves an implicit appeal to what might fully determine a theory or language. He considers that this could only be the 'sensory bombardment' to which we are subjected. His problems arise precisely because scientific theories and languages go beyond this in what they posit. Quine leaves empiricism far enough behind to allow this. He does not make the *meaning* of theories depend wholly on the observations which give rise to them. Theories can and do posit unobservable entities. Yet Quine will always emphasize the importance of the empirical base. Indeterminacy arises just because different theories rest on the same base.

No-one would suggest that observations, and experiences generally, are irrelevant to scientific theory. The difference between the empiricist and the realist can be summarized by saying that for the former experience provides the meaning of the theory. What lies beyond experience is therefore meaningless. The realist, on the other hand, does not value experience for its own sake, but only because it provides access to the rest of reality. He accepts that experiences are themselves part of reality, but he is usually more interested in what our experiences are of than in the experiences themselves. This lies behind the distinction between intersubjectivity and strong objectivity. Similar experiences can produce agreement. They can be repeated in similar situations and can possess sufficient invariance to form the base of theory or the start of language. For people to understand each other and know what they are talking about, it will be enough for each to have similar experiences in the relevant circumstances. There is no need for them to see reality as it is.

Similarity of experience is a much more important factor for communication than any requirement that experience should actually reflect the nature of reality. Indeed, let us suppose that some omniscient being did experience reality as it is. He would not be better fitted to communicate with others just because he was right and possessed infinitely superior knowledge. His superiority would make him less able to understand and be understood by others whose experiences were less rich. In fact, they could all be badly mistaken, but if they were mistaken *in the same way,* understanding would not be impeded. In this sense, intersubjective agreement guarantees understanding and translation between languages in a way in which knowledge of reality cannot. Of course, in an ideal world, the two would go together, and knowledge of reality would coincide with what people agreed amongst themselves.

Any attempt to prise knowledge apart from intersubjective agreement will instantly arouse the spectre of scepticism. How can we be sure we ever have access to reality, if we can all agree on the basis of similar experience and yet be mistaken? This is not an idle worry, and any philosophical position which rules scepticism out by definition is succumbing to an understandable temptation. There is a substantial problem here, but a refusal even to countenance the possibility of scepticism must involve the jettisoning of the idea of strong objectivity. The consequence must be the anthropocentricity which insists that knowledge is just a construct from what we all think. In Quine's case, he defines knowledge in terms of science, although he would admit that he does this from the standpoint of a particular conceptual scheme. In turn, science is made to rest on intersubjective agreement derived from experience.

Quine's views can provide for translation and yet rule out any fundamental scepticism, because he is concerned with intersubjectivity and not strong objectivity. The realism which impels him to recognize the existence of the theoretical entities of physics is a qualified realism. He still adheres to the empiricist preference for intersubjective agreement arising from sensory stimulation. His emphasis on 'indeterminacy' does not arise from any aspect of realism, but comes from his basic view that the only genuine source of determination for a theory is sensory. He has apparently loosened the ties of empiricism, so that he can entertain the possibility of referring to unobservables. Such talk, however, in a sense outstrips justification for him. The whole-hearted realist, on the other hand, would feel that his positing of entities was fully justified if the entities did in fact exist.

The full implications of Quine's predicament now emerge. We can only use our own present theory (or conceptual scheme), and whatever we say is an expression of that theory. We can only talk about reality as we conceive it, never as it is. Furthermore, the meaning of reality-as-we-conceive-it is related to the empirical base. Quine follows Duhem in looking at a theory as a whole and testing it against experience, rather than testing the different parts (or sentences) of a theory piecemeal. He can in this way espouse the verification theory of meaning, so that meaning and not just truth is related to our means of verification, and still allow for theoretical sentences about matters which cannot be directly verified. He is able to say the following:[17]

> If we recognize with Peirce that the meaning of a sentence turns purely on what would count as evidence for its truth, and if we recognize with Duhem that theoretical sentences have their evidence not as single sentences but only as larger blocks of theory, then the indeterminacy of translation of theoretical sentences is the natural conclusion.

The only evidence admissible is straightforwardly empirical, given the verification theory of meaning, and, as we have seen, Quine believes that this can support rival theories. He faces the obvious complaint that if theories share the same empirical meaning, their difference is purely verbal. His reply[18] is that 'this argument simply rules out, by definition, the doctrine that physical theory is underdetermined by all possible observation'. The Duhemian thesis that theories can only be treated as wholes enables him to go beyond the available evidence in this manner, while still believing that only experience can be the source of meaning for sentences. His realism concerning theoretical entities must be seen in the context of verificationism. The combination of the two provides Quine's philosophy with a subtle twist, but at root he accepts that linguistic meaning is associated with observation. Some sentences are 'keyed directly to observation',[19] and they are both the 'starting points in the learning of language' and 'the starting points and the check points of scientific theory'. This may seem uncontroversial, but Quine does not merely say that language or science could not get started without intersubjective observability. He ties the *meaning* of sentences to the way in which they would be collectively verified. He does not just entertain a verification theory of truth and say that the truth of a sentence is connected with our ability to recognize what makes them true. A consequence of that would be the kind of view held by Dummett, according to which a sentence may be meaningful and yet neither true nor false. Quine follows the tradition which tied not just truth but meaning as well to experience. A sentence, or block of sentences, wholly concerned with matters beyond experience would not be accepted as intelligible. The range of accepted sentences would have to be linked to the same kind of conditions which make language-learning possible in the first place.

A realist theory of meaning is complicated to devise. Our intuitions incline us to accept that meaning has to be linked in some way with experience, even if not as rigidly as the verificationists would have us believe. Yet realism demands that we sometimes talk about what lies beyond our experience, or refer to something which may be very different from the way we conceive it. It may sometimes have to be content with the affirmation that there are things beyond our experience which we may one day be in a position to talk about. It does not restrict what exists to what we are now in a position to say exists. Realism must also allow for the possibility of mistake. We may succeed in referring to something even if 'it' is later found to be very different from the way we conceived it. Reference may be tied more to our intentions than to the accuracy of what we say. This is the edge of a vast subject.[20] We must here be content to note that Quine's view that it is more important to relate word to word and translate theory into theory than to relate either to the world is evidence of his penchant for verification. He not only wants to start from where we are. He wants to stop there too. Everything has to be understood in ways which make the best possible sense of all our experiences. We have to understand different theories in terms of our own. Reference to 'the world' is ignored, for the familiar reason that we can only refer to it through our conceptual scheme. He therefore drops any notion of 'the world' and stays with that of our inclusive theory or conceptual scheme.

The Deficiencies of Quine's Realism

We must not underestimate the attractions of Quine's doctrine, because he does try to accept many realist insights. He is no ally of Feyerabend. He does not wish to restrict the scope of truth wholly to the interior of a theory, and accepts that there is a sense in which we can speak of theories as true or false. He embraces Tarski's theory of truth, but, as we have seen, that could mean anything. The echoes from Peirce are more significant. Quine is not concerned with the metaphysical status of sentences but rather with what we can do with them. Thus 'truth' is not going to carry for him any implication of a connection with a reality beyond what we now conceive. We cannot talk of truth apart from what *we* hold true. Truth is reduced to 'what is held true', and theories cannot be said to be true or false *before* they have been adopted or rejected. We cannot stand outside two theories and judge their truth. The choice has to be made with reference to another criterion such as simplicity. Once it has been made, we can then say from the standpoint of the adopted theory that is true or false. The realist twist in this is that Quine would want to say that the truth I judge is absolute. Truth is judged from within our own overall changing system of the world, because there is no higher standard to which we can appeal. In Quine's own words,[21] truth is *immanent*, and only has life in the whole inclusive theory. Yet it is at the same time absolute. We can affirm the statements of our theory with all the conviction we may. Because we can do nothing more than that, what, Quine asks, could be more absolute? After the adoption of a theory, I am perfectly entitled to call the rejected theories mistaken or false.

Quine denies he is lowering his sights and settling for a relativistic doctrine of truth. He says:[22]

> The saving consideration is that we continue to take seriously our own particular aggregate science, our own particular world-theory. . . Unlike Descartes, we own and use our beliefs at the moment. . . until by what is vaguely called scientific method we change them here and there for the better. Within our own total evolving doctrine, we can judge truth as earnestly and absolutely as can be: subject to correction, but that goes without saying.

When he talks of 'judging absolutely', Quine is referring to the attitude with which we hold a belief rather than to its 'metaphysical' status. Yet he is prejudging the issue. Why *should* we judge something 'absolutely'? What right have we to be dogmatic about our beliefs? We earlier quoted Peirce saying that instead of trying to attain 'Truth' it would be better to try for a state of mind unassailable by doubt. Quine similarly wishes to link absolute truth to the conviction with which we assent to sentences. The fact that we continue to take our inclusive theory seriously is a bulwark against relativism for him. Yet this inverts what should be the correct order. There is no doubt a link between truth and taking a theory seriously, but it is not as Quine portrays it. We do not think something is true *because* we take it seriously. It is not even the case that taking a theory seriously constitutes truth. We rather take it seriously *because* we think it true.

Quine's insistence that we can judge absolutely from within a conceptual scheme does allude to one important fact. There is no need for the total opposition between concepts and reality we have already seen sketched by some philosophers. The reality we judge may be 'our reality', but it is fallacious to conclude that reality-in-itself must be completely different and inaccessible. Our judgements may not create reality, but that does not mean that judgements and reality can never walk hand in hand. Correct judgements reflect reality and Quine's attempt to stress the immanence and yet the absolute character of the truth we judge points to this. Judgements arise from a theory and yet purport to be about something independent of theory. What we believe can never be dismissed as 'merely' our belief or 'just' an expression of our conceptual scheme. Nevertheless, Quine is right to see that although truth has to be claimed by a theory, and we have to speak from inside it, that does not mean that truth is relative to it. The origin of the claim does not affect its validity.

Quine is interested in intersubjectivity rather than strong objectivity and his emphasis on the verification theory of meaning explains this. Meaning must be tied to our experience, or, putting it more behaviouristically, since Quine has behaviourist leanings, it must be tied to the disposition of men to assent to or dissent from particular observation sentences. This provides the foundation of language in general and science in particular. His notion of objectivity is somewhat strange at first sight. It is not for him an all or nothing affair, whereas 'strong objectivity' clearly is. The way things are independently of judgements made about them cannot be something admitting of degrees. They either exist unaffected by judgements or conceptual schemes, or they do not. Quine, however, thinks that something is less objective when intersubjective agreement is in doubt. We need what he terms 'analytical hypotheses' to identify what counts as assent or dissent when we question the speaker of an alien language in our first attempts to understand him. Even when things are in front of the speaker and observation sentences are in question, a linguist cannot be utterly certain that he has correctly identified the native's reactions. There is a certain amount of indeterminacy even at the very beginning. Quine uses the term 'stimulus meaning' to sum up a subject's disposition to assent to or dissent from observation sentences. He admits that we cannot be absolutely certain that we have obtained a perfect match between the native's language and our own. While stimulus meaning can be properly looked upon[23] as 'the objective reality a linguist has to probe', such meaning is only objective relative to a linguist's identification of assent as assent. There is that much less objectivity because analytical hypotheses are necessary. Translation has to be built on foundations in which indeterminacy is an inevitable part. In Quine's system, objectivity is determined by what is intersubjectively available.

The main strategy which Quine pursues is to start from the impact of the external world on our sensory organs and to see how we can build up our theories from that basic beginning. Although theories may go beyond the evidence they are not accidental. Evolution will favour some rather than others. He comments that 'man and other animals are body-minded by natural selection',[24] and would admit that even this remark is the expression of current scientific theory. Nevertheless, despite the fact that we can only approach reality through theory, the reality posited by theory is not part of it or dependent on it. Quine would say that his theory of the world gives preference to the physical world, while the idealist gives preference to evidence. Given that we have an atomic theory, atoms are to be considered real and not as mere reflections of the theory.

What more could a realist want? The constant reiteration of the fact that we can only speak through our conceptual scheme is a truism. As Putnam has commented:[25] 'Well. We should use *someone else's* conceptual system?' Granted that this is a truism and that truth is immanent to theory, Quine's acceptance of the absolute nature of the truth claimed within a theory seems enough to satisfy a realist. Or does it? Although the whole doctrine is exceedingly subtle and accommodating, doubts remain. One difficulty is that the bounds of reality seem set by the current state of scientific theory. Quine is very insistent that there is at least one fact of the matter beyond theory. There is no 'first philosophy'. Epistemology does not lie beyond science, sitting in judgement on it, but merely falls into place as 'a chapter of psychology and hence of natural science'.[26] The present state of science becomes the arbiter of what there is. Such an approach does not always seems to take seriously the limitations of science, and the possibility that we may learn about reality from other sources. The dogmatic rejection of an epistemology superior to science also invites the question how such a view could itself be substantiated. Is it verifiable, and, if not, what is its status?

There are deeper reasons for concern. Putting aside Quine's devotion to science, his method is inevitably anthropocentric. What man can say about reality may be limited to what man can say about reality, but the self-subsistence of that reality must not be ignored. Quine can retort that our theories posit it as self-subsistent, but we can still wonder about the status of those unknown parts of reality not yet captured by our scientific theories. He thinks that the underdetermination of theory will always be with us. We have already noted his rejection of Peirce's notion of one ideal limit for science. He says:[27] 'The totality of possible observations of nature, made and unmade, is compatible with physical theories that are incompatible with each other.' We never will reach a state when we can talk of what reality is like, except from the standpoint of one amongst several possible theories. Once we accept that when all possible observations are made, we still are going to have competing theories and are denied access to reality, Quine's realism gains a very peculiar tinge. In the last resort, there may still be different realities posited by different theories. They will each rest on the same empirical base, and yet there will be indeterminacy of translation between them. As a result, we will not even be able to tell how far they are mutually incompatible, and indeed we can call them different theories only relative to some analytical hypotheses for translation between them.

One way of looking at theories would be to see them as attempts at characterizing reality which have to be modified as knowledge increases. When we finally achieve full knowledge, we would be able to leave mere theory behind. If theory is contrasted with knowledge in this manner, we can say that Quine's doctrine is deficient because it never allows us to go beyond theory. Of course, the very possibility of being able to do so is in question. Quine does not even believe that one of the final competing theories will be the correct one, although we shall not be in a position even then to judge which it is. He cannot allow that there is *any* sense in talking of right or wrong here, except from a vantage point within one of the theories. The verification theory of meaning ensures that whatever is meaningfully claimed and whatever can be understood must be related to observation. When all possible observations are accounted for, nothing more could make an intelligible difference. Nothing can decide between the competing theories *ex hypothesi* left in the ring. Although they may each posit different entities, there is no sense, it seems, in saying that the entities in the world must be as one theory rather than another says, nor is there room for the sceptical worry that *all* the theories may be wrong. We may think it a gain that radical scepticism cannot get a footing, but, in Quine's case, this gain has been produced at the cost of making 'the world' and 'reality' theoretical terms. As such, they form a barrier which can never be surmounted.

One of the difficulties about looking at Quine's philosophy from a realist point of view is that there is a sense in which

Quine will agree with everything the realist may wish to say. The qualification will be that Quine will insist that the realist is only making his remarks within the context of some overall theory of the world. This is why the attempted interpretation of one theory of objects in terms of another is important. It is the only way of talking about them, other than by reiterating the original theory. Reference is never allowed by Quine to break out into 'reality as it is'. He would not find the latter phrase intelligible.

It is perhaps inevitable that a preoccupation with semantic notions in language will be biased against a realist view, although we have seen that language can include a realist emphasis, since the distinction between truth conditions and verification conditions can be stated within a language. Yet a deeper worry remains. Concentration on linguistic meaning and translation may be important, but when one tries to conceive of reality exclusively through language, it is not surprising that its limitations restrict one's view of reality. Reality as described by human language need not exhaust all there is, any more than the universe necessarily corresponds to the present state of science. Scientists cannot go beyond the present state of knowledge in their accounts of what there is, but that does not mean that they remain content with it. Neither language nor science is static, and philosophic views must take account of linguistic innovation and scientific progress. Quine would claim he does just that, but he removes the goal at which anyone aims who wants to understand the world. A complete and unique understanding is made impossible in principle.

Reality must be the same to all who have access to it, if it is self-subsistent. Even if it were in fact a shapeless chaos, everyone not in error would discover that to be so. Strong objectivity implies the possibility of intersubjectively shared knowledge. This is not to say that everyone will see things from the same perspective. Different sensory organs or different instruments will obviously make a difference to how something is perceived. Yet the object of perception or experiment will remain the same. A realist must accept that a convergence of scientific knowledge should in principle occur. In the end, different scientific theories will have to mesh in with each other or be rejected. Peirce was right to think of an ideal limit to science, however hypothetical. He did not see clearly that, far from providing an empiricist substitute for a metaphysical view of thing-in-themselves, such a conception *follows* from the nature of reality. If there is *one* reality common to all theories and portrayed in a better or worse fashion in each, that provides the ideal limit for science. Quine's rejection of the notion of one terminus for all scientific theory and his insistence on its underdetermination is the natural outcome of the verification theory of meaning. What is not intelligible to man because of its connection with sensory experience must be ruled out. Yet this shows that Quine has lost his grasp on the notion of a single common reality as the subject matter of language and science. He starts with man and is always kept within the levels of what men think real or hold true. His conclusion may have been different if he had started with reality, even if it only had the status for him of a regulative concept.

Quine could retort that a realist theory is as much a theory of reality, underdetermined by the evidence, as any other. The view that reality is independent of theory and common to all theories is itself a theory. Since it is what we are saying about reality, there is some truth in this. Yet if men are forever boxed in by their own conceptions and unable to grasp external reality, we end up with the very idealist position of sticking to the evidence, which Quine in fact rejects. We have noted that in his rejection of 'first philosophy', and in his adoption of the verification theory of meaning, he is not afraid to say certain things absolutely. The verification theory of meaning, even if sparingly applied, results in an undue narrowing of attention to public behaviour. Quine inevitably concentrates on dispositions to overt behaviour and treats language as a behavioural response to publicly checkable stimuli. His theory of language is one of stimulus and response. 'The fixed points', he says,[28] 'are just the shared stimulus and the word.' Indeed even theory for him is merely a body of sentences. He has no truck with such subtleties as intentions to refer, where we did not succeed. He says[29] that 'the easy familiarity of mentalistic talk is not to be trusted'. After reality has been limited to what man can talk about, we find that what man can talk about is limited to what is in front of him or to theories he can build as a consequence of what is in front of him.

The verificationist's demand for what can be publicly checked may restrict our vision excessively. It may well, though, have its roots in the correct idea that reality, whatever form it might take, is open to all and the same for all. The verificationist wants to make life easy by making reality more accessible than it really is. There is indeed a sense in which reality for the verificationist *is* just what is public and checkable, often merely according to the present state of science. It can take on a highly parochial tinge. Quine's adoption of the verification theory of meaning is tempered by his application of it to whole blocks of sentences and not to individual ones. Nevertheless when objectivity is taken to imply intersubjective accessibility, objective reality can only consist of shared stimuli and people's reports of them. These form the bedrock of Quine's philosophy.

The Possibility of a Unique Description of the World

The underdetermination of our theory of nature is not the explanation of the indeterminacy of translation. Quine emphasizes[30] that the latter would still remain even if we possess the 'whole truth about nature'. This raises the question whether even given a fully realistic conception of 'the world' we are right to insist on one ideal limit in science. Is there in principle only one conceptual framework which will reflect the world? Putting problems of underdetermination on one side, how can we be sure that we may not, even in the end, have a choice of concepts each of which would capture reality as it is? Even granted full knowledge of the world, we may still have a choice of which entities to talk about. To take Quine's example, some cultures may pick out rabbits, while others will prefer to talk in terms of unde-tached rabbit parts. Yet all will be talking of the same world. Is the realist entitled to insist that only one description is right and that they are, in fact, *rabbits*? Quine would say 'no, there is no real question of right choice'. One complication is that this is not an example where people are genuinely contradicting each other. It is not like an argument about whether or not there are electrons. There the realist would be perfectly justified in saying that one side must be right and the other wrong. There cannot both be and not be electrons. In the 'rabbit' case, it is clear that there can be both rabbits and undetached rabbit parts. It follows that there are rabbit parts, if there are rabbits. Both sides are merely drawing attention to different aspects of the same world in a way that is peculiarly difficult to unmask. Quine is deliberately running together what people are referring to and how it is possible to find out what they are referring to. He is not saying just that the evidence does not determine which theory is correct, but also that it cannot even determine the correct translation of what another speaker is saying.

Both references to rabbits and to undetached rabbit parts occurs in virtue of the same facts. Each provides equivalent descriptions of the same part of the world. The realist has to face the question whether even if there is general agreement about the nature of the world, he wants to demand more. Does he want to insist that there is only *one* correct way of describing the world? This is a deeper point than one about an ideal limit to science. It would seem to follow that science can only give one basic account of the world, if the world has a single nature. Yet is there room within that account for alternative equivalent descriptions, or is one of them always going to be the basic one? Could we be right in our intuition that, whatever other ways there may be of dividing the world up, there are really rabbits? The little furry creatures might be seen as basic units which are there whether we choose to notice them or not. Those who only refer to rabbit parts may not be fully seeing the world as it is, even though they are picking out what is there.

Putnam is certain that the possibility of giving equivalent descriptions is not inconsistent with realism. He says flatly :[31] 'A twentieth century realist cannot ignore the existence of equivalent descriptions: realism is not committed to there being one true theory (and *only* one).'

He goes on to draw an analogy between equivalent descriptions and the alternative mappings (mercator, polar etc.) of the earth which are available to a geographer. Certainly a map is to some extent an imperfect representation of reality. What makes the map accurate is totally independent of the map. The shape of the world and the position of the continents is not affected by the activity of geographers. There are nevertheless different ways of projecting a three-dimensional world on to paper. The only completely accurate mapping would involve a full-scale replica, and any scaling down or portrayal in two dimensions will demand greater interpretation. Different projections, when interpreted, will give knowledge of the same reality. They may involve alternative methods of mapping but they are accurate, or inaccurate, in virtue of the same world. This latter point may be all the realist requires. He does not need to adjudicate between different positions, each of which may have its strengths and weaknesses.

Are we, therefore, to say that there is one world and only one actual combination of entities, but that there may be equivalent descriptions of it which cannot be reduced to each other's terms? There seems to be no reason why we may not have two ways of dividing up the world simultaneously, and know that they are each referring to the same reality. Must we in principle be able to say that one is better than the other? A geographer could certainly compare different map projections without having to conclude that one was *the* correct one. They are all correct within the limits they set themselves. Yet it is because two-dimensional projections are trying to do what is strictly impossible for them when mapping three-dimensional reality that we have to settle for alternatives. No-one would find it helpful to build a replica world, but that is in principle the best way of mapping our present one without distortion. Small-scale three-dimensional globes are also perhaps less misleading than printed maps. We are wrong in meekly accepting that two-dimensional mappings are accurate. They are helpful according to their lights, but the possibility of alternative projections may itself be a symptom of their basic inadequacy.

Application of this illustration to the relationship of conceptual schemes with reality gives little encouragement to the view that there may be equivalent and equally correct portrayals of reality. Such a position is a realist one, but there seems no reason why this is in principle all we can hope for. The nature of concepts, or of language, might make them intrinsically inadequate to express what is the case, but it could surely also be maintained that scientists, at least, should not be content until they have arrived at a unique description of the world. Such a position would fill the regulative role of spurring scientists on and not allowing them to rest content too soon. It is not obvious that it is pointless to wonder whether rabbits or undetached rabbit parts are more fundamental. Different cultural backgrounds may lead groups to notice different elements of objective reality. Nevertheless this is explicable in terms of their culture and has nothing directly to do with the nature of what they observe. When a culture is idiosyncratic enough to think that undetached rabbit parts are more important biologically than the whole rabbit, a realist is at liberty to say not just that this is a different way of viewing the same features of the world, but that it is an inadequate way. Different conceptual schemes may 'map' the same reality, but this is evidence of some defect in them. Full knowledge must be tied to a unique conceptual scheme. Whether it is attainable in any given area must be a separate question.

Equivalent Descriptions and Relativity

One place in which it might seem appropriate to talk of 'equivalent descriptions' is in the context of views about relativity in physics, such as those of Einstein. Reichenbach remarks[32] that 'the word "relativity" should be interpreted as meaning "relative to a certain definitional system"' and he says the following:

> The definitional character of fundamental concepts leads to a plurality of equivalent descriptions. A familiar illustration is given by the various descriptions of motion resulting when the system regarded as being at rest is varied. Another illustration is presented by the various geometries resulting, for the same physical space, through changes in the definition of congruence. All these different descriptions represent different languages saying the same thing; equivalent descriptions, therefore, express the same physical content.

He goes on to remark that relativity does not mean an abandonment of truth, but only that truth can be formulated in various ways. He gives as a simple example the fact that two statements 'the room is twenty-one feet long' and 'the room is seven yards long' say the same thing. It all depends on the unit of measurement one chooses. They are both true in virtue of the same fact, and it would seem perverse to maintain that one is more accurate than the other. In the same way, it is alleged, questions about space and time depend on the coordinate system chosen, and there is thus in some areas no such thing as one uniquely correct description. There are just different, but empirically equivalent descriptions, depending on different frames of reference. The basic physical laws, however, are invariant and it is precisely because of this that relativity follows in some contexts. Margeneau gives as an example the fact that the basic laws of electrodynamics involve the speed of light, c. He says:[33]

If these laws are to be invariant, c must be constant. But

the constancy of c in different inertial systems requires
that moving objects contract, that moving clocks be
retarded, that there can be no universal simultaneity,
and so forth. To achieve *objectivity* of basic description,
the theory must confer relativity upon the domain of
immediate observations.

The frame of reference adopted will govern how one
describes what is happening, but the reality described and the
laws governing its behaviour will be the same for all. We may
arrive at different accounts of motion by regarding different
systems as being at rest, but the situation described in
different ways is independent of the descriptions. *All* equivalent descriptions which seemed true would prove equally
false, if we were shown to be under a misapprehension about
it. The descriptions appear equivalent precisely because they
are about the same happenings. Relativity in this context does
not undermine objectivity. It depends on it. Yet does not this
tell against our previous remarks which denied the possibility
of alternative, equally correct, views of reality? The ability to
describe the same event using different frames of reference,
none of which can be thought *the* correct one, seems to
provide an example of precisely this. It does at one level, but
talk of relativity depends on a more general theory about
reality, and *that* is most certainly not just one of a number of
equally good theories. Either it is an adequate one or it is not.

An analogy can be drawn with the way the same mountain
can look very different from different vantage points. We
cannot go on to say how it *really* looks, since that all depends
on the position of the observer. Its nature is, however,
invariant and totally independent of observation. There may
be several equally good places from which to see it, but that
does not suggest the mountain itself *is* different depending on
how one sees it. Its single character is precisely what gives
rise to different perceptions of it. In the same way, the
important feature of relativity is not so much the different
descriptions, which may be available in the relevant circum-

stances, as the features which remain invariant and which enable us to see that certain desciptions *are* equivalent and *are* equally valid. As Margeneau says, 'the idea of invariance is the nucleus of the theory of relativity'.

Some theoretical statements have to hold in all contexts and cannot be replaced by others. The notion of equivalent descriptions can only hold when we have some unique standard by which to decide *which* descriptions are equivalent and which are not. It must remain a subsidiary notion. Our ability to equate seven yards with twenty-one feet is closely connected with our use of either measurement in picking out objects of the same length. Without an ability on our part to refer to physical objects, the concept of equal length would have no application. Descriptions are equivalent because they are about the same segment of reality. Yet this cannot mean that there must be some unique way of picking out the very events which can be described in alternative ways. That seems to involve the impossible task of stepping outside all reference frames. At the same time, it seems absurd to suppose that one reference frame should be thought *the* right one.

There may be an apparent dilemma here, but it is not a genuine one. The comparison between the equivalent descriptions allowed by relativity theory, and the possibility of alternative, equivalent ways of carving up the world and theorizing about it, is faulty. The theory of relativity tells us how things are, if it is correct, and as a result our views about what is invariant have to change. As a result, too, we can use independent criteria to judge which descriptions are equivalent. The possibility of alternative descriptions of reality is analogous to, and indeed is the same question as whether the theory of relativity is just one of a number of equally good ways of talking about reality. It is not analogous to the consequences which occur within the theory. We would be sawing off the branch we are sitting on, if we concluded that we may legitimately regard the nature of reality in different but equivalent ways, on the basis of what happens in the theory of relativity. We would be assuming the unique truth of the theory and its consequences in order to say that because of them we cannot maintain there is any unique way of describing reality completely accurately. The possibility of one conceptual scheme reflecting reality is not denied by modern physics. It is an essential precondition if the work of scientists is to progress.

4 REALITY AND ALTERNATIVE CONCEPTUAL SCHEMES

The Dualism of Subject and Object

The matching of man's conceptual scheme with reality involves juggling with what are apparently two items. 'Mind' and 'the world' provide one example of how these have been understood, and the idealist answer was that the two items are really one. 'The world' is a construction out of mind. The realist must hold that there are two items, and it is hardly surprising that anti-realists will sometimes claim that this is an illusion. There is not much agreement about how the items are to be categorized. Quine substitutes language for mind, and sensory evidence for 'the world', and the problem can also be described by simply referring to 'subject' and 'object'. Even if we stick to the vague formulation of concepts and reality, it is evident that many problems do not arise because of the kind of categories used, but rather because there are *two* of them. The problem of underdetermination is inevitable for Quine because he is trying to fit theories to sensory evidence when the theories themselves go far beyond the evidence. Idealism is attractive when it seems as if one of the two items that must be matched is forever inaccessible.

Why should the realist insist that there are two items? The whole point of realism is that it insists on the self-subsistence of the reality in question. The *raison d'être* of science is to investigate something independent of the process of investigation. There are endless complications when the activity of scientists itself affects the object of investigation, and even then their task is to understand the nature of the reality concerned apart from their interference. From the realist point of view, any blurring of the distinction between the investigator and his method of research, on the one hand, and the object of study on the other, will merely make the investigation pointless.

Realism and anti-realism fight each other in a variety of contexts, and it is no sign of inconsistency to refuse to hand a blank cheque to realism. 'Strong objectivity' may not obtain in all quarters. The objects of science, however, provide a test case, and it is difficult to envisage realism being able to sustain attacks in other areas if it can be vanquished in science. The scientist and his activity must be logically distinct from the object of his study. What is the case is so whether or not it is perceived or measured. The view that reality is in principle common to everyone, even if they sometimes see different aspects of it, also leads to the same conclusion. Any blurring of the distinction between subject and object, so that they become, as it were, a single entity, entails that we cannot refer to 'the same object' as other subjects. Each subject-object amalgam will inevitably become a distinct unit, with no such thing as an 'object' apart from a 'subject'. When this is applied to concepts and reality, the view that there are different amalgams if there are different concepts entails that reality can no longer be thought of as common and external to all conceptual schemes.

This raises the problem of the possibility of alternative conceptual schemes. Even if we leave aside the inconsistencies of relativism, there is a deeper problem. Many would deny that the notion of an alternative conceptual scheme was intelligible. The denial of realism does not, though, inevitably lead to the conclusion that there will be many conceptual schemes, with no way of deciding between them. Similarly, it does not follow from realism that there will in fact be only one conceptual scheme. There may in principle be only one absolutely *correct* one, but that is a different matter. There are many ways of being mistaken.

Genuine realism cannot allow for any influence on reality

by the subject in so far as he possesses knowledge. This is not underwriting a belief in the total passivity of mind, or underestimating the role of concepts in categorizing and selecting. Our expectations often govern what we notice, and our present conceptual scheme doubtless often ensures that we see one thing rather than another. We are not suggesting, either, that reality is static. The point is simply that once massive interaction is envisaged between knower and reality, the boundaries become blurred and eventually vanish. This may seem a surprising generalization, since it is a matter of normal experience that we interact with our environment. We affect it and it affects us. This is irrelevant to the logical relationship between knowing subject and what is known. The status of knowledge itself is in jeopardy when the distinction between these items is blurred. Reality does not alter merely because we obtain knowledge of it. If it did, we could never know what it was like before we knew it. Reality as it is in itself, unaffected by commerce with a knowing subject, would be inaccessible to us. We could no longer conceive of reality but only of various subject-object combinations. Only the distinct nature of reality makes shared knowledge possible.

Various causal relationships can occur between knowing subject and object. Some philosophers indeed would claim that knowledge itself is causally produced. Nothing we are saying precludes the possibility that a subject can causally influence an object. He may not be able to obtain knowledge without interfering with the object in a way which subsequently alters it. This kind of causal interaction is not in any way comparable with the conceptual relation between knower and object known. Attempts to amalgamate the latter put the possibility of knowledge in question by reducing the two items to one. Reference to a causal relation demands the existence of two separate items. There could be no causal interaction if subject and object were indistinguishable.

The positivist's reduction of scientific theory to accounting for actual and possible sensations can be seen as a reduction of the realist's two items to one. Reality becomes the observations made, and the knowing subjects who make the observations merely systematize them. Theory and observation are not logically distinct. The former can never outstrip the latter. The positivist may be particularly concerned to guarantee intersubjectivity, but his rejection of entities beyond observation ensures that strong objectivity is impossible. There are many similarities between this position and idealism, where knowledge of the object ultimately replaces the object, even though idealism seems very 'metaphysical' compared with positivism's tough-minded rejection of anything beyond the scope of science. Even the most rabid empiricist, however, can draw attention to one duality. He may have given up the notion of unexperienced reality, but he has replaced it with that of experience, and he still has the task of fitting his conceptual scheme, or his language, to experience. This is why empiricism seems very concerned with objectivity. It may reject strong objectivity, but it can still provide a surrogate for reality in the form of the notion of empirical content. A good theory will maximize empirical content and a meaningless theory will have none. Language may only be about actual or possible sensory experience, but at least it seems to be *about* something.

Even this dualism is called into question by some philosophers, such as Donald Davidson. They fear any distinction between conceptual scheme and uninterpreted experience. The same argument would apply to scheme and uninterpreted reality too, and realist views would be as much the object of attack as an empiricist's. Such philosophers think that once scheme and content are cut adrift from each other, and have to be fitted together, the spectre of alternative conceptual frameworks raises itself. People are then free to organize reality, or their experience, differently. The realist may not worry about this possibility as long as the reality being organized is understood to be accessible by all systems. Similarly the empiricist must consider that experience, observation, sensory promptings, or whatever, are independent of all conceptual schemes and the basis of them all. Many putting forward the possibility of alternative conceptual framworks would not accept this, but would make what was to count as reality or experience an internal matter for their theory or framework. There would be no bedrock common to all schemes.

The very idea of an alternative conceptual framework is a slippery one. What precisely is it? It is possible to envisage different frameworks dividing the same reality up differently, but in a way intelligible to those who do not share the framework. Divisions between colours, for instance, could be drawn differently in different systems and yet it would be perfectly possible for the adherents of each to learn the distinctions made by the other merely by looking at the groupings of coloured objects each made. On the other hand, an alternative conceptual framework could be envisaged as totally inaccessible to outsiders. It might, for instance, be the kind of thing which Martians or creatures from even more remote regions might possess. If they had different perceptual equipment, it might be very difficult and perhaps impossible to understand what they were saying. Even in this case, though, the fact that we all had access to the same world might provide a starting point for understanding. Even if they perceived things differently, a realist can assume that *what* they are seeing is identical for each of us. In the same way that different senses can all give us information about the same object, creatures with senses which we have not got could be assumed to be perceiving the objects we do and perhaps gaining information which is not available to us.

There is something of a dilemma apparent in dealing with the possibility of alternative frameworks. If they are inter-translatable, they might not seem genuine alternatives at all. If, on the other hand, they each have concepts not possessed by the other, and they cannot be correlated, it is not obvious that the adherents of the one will ever be able to understand the other. Davidson has written:[1]

> The failure of intertranslatability is a necessary condition for difference of conceptual schemes: the common relation to experience or the evidence is what is supposed to help us make sense of the claim that it is languages or schemes that are under consideration when translation fails. It is essential to this idea that there be something neutral and common that lies outside all schemes.

Davidson wishes to argue that the 'dualism of scheme and content, or organizing system and something waiting to be organized, cannot be made intelligible and defensible'. He dismisses it as a dogma of empiricism, and quite mistakenly takes the views of Kuhn and Feyerabend to be examples of this dualism. Yet the whole trouble[2] with their views is that they did not have any clear notion of anything external to the system. Davidson is on firmer ground in holding up the views of Quine as an example. As we have seen the dualism between sensory experience and conceptual scheme is very much a feature of his doctrine.

Davidson will have nothing to do with the idea of any neutral content waiting to be organized, and thinks that it leads to conceptual relativism. He is right to feel uneasy, in so far as this invites the prospect of different conceptual schemes with no way of correlating them. The idealist has traditionally thought that minds would agree about the conceptual scheme they produced. When idealist criticisms of realism are upheld together with a blithe acceptance that schemes may differ, we are in trouble. Any point of contact between schemes seems lost. One response to this is the slippery slope to relativism and on to nihilism. We can shrug our shoulders and say that it does not matter how we think. Another is to deny the intelligibility of the notion of different conceptual schemes. For instance, Stroud echoes[3] Quine's preferences for gradual rather than systematic change, and holds that it makes no sense to talk of rejecting our conceptual schemes and choosing an alternative. He says:

We can give no content to the notion of a conceptual scheme or language which is a genuine alternative to our present one. No revision open to us can take us beyond the language we now use and understand—any 'alternative' is either something we already understand and make sense of, or it is no alternative at all.

Davidson would accept this argument which is fundamentally verificationist. What we cannot understand here and now has to be ruled out.

Davidson's 'Principle of Charity'

Davidson is particularly concerned with the problem of playing off meanings against beliefs when faced with a problem of translation or interpretation. He follows Quine in thinking that the discovery of meaning involves identifying what people are disposed to say in particular circumstances. The problem then arises that it may be difficult to see whether they have inappropriate beliefs or are using words in an unusual way. If someone reports that there is an elephant in the garden, they may be quite right, but if there is not one there, we are faced with a choice in our interpretation of what was said. They may know perfectly well what is ordinarily meant by 'elephant' and be undergoing an hallucination. In that case they would mean the same as we do by the word but have a false belief. On the other hand, they may have a perfectly correct belief about what is in the garden and yet mean by 'elephant' what we mean by 'badger'. Small children are, of course, particularly liable to this kind of confusion, but the same methodological problem arises when faced with the speech dispositions of an alien tribe. Do they see what we see and have similar beliefs to us? Any apparent awkwardness arising in translation can be traced, if they do, to problems with meaning rather than belief. If we cannot be sure of what they might believe, we cannot know whether the explanations for what they say may lie in the oddity of their belief. Davidson will not adopt any dichotomy between scheme and content because of his fear of relativism. He does not use the notion of sensory experience in his explanation of meaning. He sees that we must anchor belief in some way in order to provide some stability in the process of interpretation when we are faced with the dual problem of what someone's beliefs are and what his words mean. As a result, he stresses the crucial role played by the attitude of *holding true* or *accepting as true*, and says[4] that 'most uses of language tell us directly, or shed light on the question whether a speaker holds a sentence to be true'. We would be able to uncover the meaning of what they said in particular circumstances if we could have some indication of what the speakers of a language held true. If they uttered certain words when it was raining, and we could be reasonably sure that they would accept as true that it was raining, then we could conclude that that would be the meaning of their utterance.

Davidson himself points out that we must not assume that people never have false beliefs. He comments: 'Error is what gives belief its point.' The whole process of interpretation, though, seems in jeopardy if we entertain the possibility of massive error. Too many false beliefs about something undermine 'the validity of the description of the belief as being about that subject'. Davidson's own rather startling example is that of the ancients who believed that the earth was flat. This is a favourite example used by philosophers when they want to point to an obviously false belief. Yet Davidson queries whether the belief is false, or at least whether we can be sure it is. The problem he has posed should lead us to wonder whether we are playing meaning off correctly with false belief. Perhaps we are too ready to identify a belief as one about *that* object. We may be faced not with a silly belief about it but with a true belief about a different one. Davidson therefore asks whether the ancients believed *this* earth was flat. He says:[5]

Well, this earth of ours is part of the solar system, a system partly identified by the fact that it is a gaggle of large cool, solid, bodies circling around a very large, hot star. If someone believes *none* of this about the earth, is it certain that it is the earth he is thinking of? An answer is not called for. The point is made if this kind of consideration of related beliefs can shake one's confidence that the ancients believed the earth was flat.

There must come a time, he feels, when cumulative error undermines any chance that someone can be understood to be talking about this rather than that thing. The choice between their being very wrong about the one thing rather than more correct about something else becomes impossible. We can never get to grips with the meaning of what they say, unless we can make some assumptions about their beliefs. As a result, Davidson thinks it necessary that interpretation should rule out the possibility of massive error. He says: 'A theory of interpretation cannot be correct that makes a man assent to very many false sentences: it must generally be the case that a sentence is true when a speaker holds it to be.' The speaker or the interpreter can be wrong: neither are infallible. Davidson wishes to aim at a *general* agreement of belief between interpreter and speaker. If sentences are generally true when speakers hold them to be, we can assume that agreement between speakers is not only desirable but essential. Since most of my beliefs are true, and most of yours as well, a correct translation will be bound to uncover a considerable correspondence between beliefs. Doubt is cast on the translation when too much apparent disagreement is revealed.

Davidson holds that the concepts of objective truth and error emerge as we interpret belief. He emphasizes the distinction between 'a sentence being held true and being in fact true', and for him this is just the distinction between an individual's belief and the 'public norm provided by language'. Because of his opposition to the attempt to match two separate items, he cannot allow that truth lies in the relationship between language and any neutral uninterpreted reality. Truth arises from what is generally agreed. The effect of his ruling that most of our beliefs must be true is to close any possible gap between concepts or beliefs on the one hand and reality on the other. We have to assume that other people are right in most of their beliefs, just as most of ours must be true. We have to operate with a 'principle of charity'. Davidson comments: 'Charity is forced on us: whether we like it or not, if we want to understand others, we must count them right in most matters.' When they hold a sentence true in particular, observed circumstances, we have to take it as *prima facie* evidence that it is true in these circumstances. If a German says 'Es schneit' and we see that he only says it when confronted with snow, we can assume that it means the same as the words 'It is snowing' uttered by English speakers in these circumstances.

Davidson thus hopes to achieve an understanding of meaning and translation by assuming a prior grasp of the concept of truth. It appears that we can uncover the meaning of what people say when we know what they are likely to hold true. We must as a general principle, therefore, look for truth in other people's talk. He says:[6]

> Widespread agreement is the only possible background against which disputes and mistakes can be interpreted. Making sense of the utterances and behaviour of others, even their most aberrant behaviour, requires us to find a great deal of reason and truth in them. To see too much unreason on the part of others is simply to undermine our ability to understand what it is they are so unreasonable about.

This dismissal *a priori* of far-reaching error may make translation possible, but it seems far too easy a way of dealing with traditional sceptical worries. Can most people really be assumed to be right on most matters? Such a view seems to take the possibility of mistake too lightly. It demands that everything be understood in terms of our current conceptual scheme, or else be dismissed as meaningless. Yet we do not have to be sceptics to start wondering whether we may not be hugely mistaken in some of our beliefs. General agreement may be a guide to truth but it does not constitute it. Davidson cannot distinguish between what is generally held true and what is true, although he allows for mistakes and accepts that in a minority of cases what is held true need not be true. This is hardly surprising when he has ruled out any link between true sentences and something outside all conceptual schemes. He has nothing left to appeal to apart from the judgements which are actually made.

It is undoubtedly a precondition for understanding that we assume that people have similar beliefs in similar situations. Teaching or learning a language would be impossible if pupil and teacher were unable to assume that they were each talking about the same things. Yet does this mean that things must actually be as we conceive them, or is it merely necessary that everyone have similar beliefs in particular circumstances? Of course, questions about whether it is snowing can hardly be lumped together with problems concerning sub-atomic particles. There is far less room for error in the former case. Yet even in cases of putative snow, the word can be taught merely if both parties believe it is snowing. They will know what they are talking about, as long as each undergoes the same illusion. There is no need to add the further requirement that it actually be snowing. The best explanation for the similarity of people's experience is that they are all experiencing the same thing, but language teaching progresses through our experience and not through the way things are. This leaves open the possibility that reality may be different from our conception of it. Davidson's arguments suggest that if we are to understand another language, most of the beliefs expressed in it should be similar to ours. His demand that most beliefs should be *true* is in fact additional to this. It no doubt follows that if my beliefs are mostly true and yours are too, then we shall hold the majority of our beliefs in common, but this latter is all that is necessary for mutual understanding. We can talk to each other about snow if I believe it is snowing when you do. Whether 'snow' really refers to anything in the external world and our beliefs are true is a further problem.

It may be important in understanding what is said by the speakers of an alien language to be able to identify what is held true by them. An obvious way of doing this is to look for similarities between what they and we hold true. The assumptions that these similarities will be there is what makes the task of radical translation possible. An objection may be raised that the very identification of what is held true relies on the prior identification of the circumstances in which the beliefs occur. It is all very well accepting that there will be a correspondence of belief between aliens and ourselves, but it will be pointed out that this can only be discovered by looking at particular circumstances and knowing what we hold true about them. We can then assume that aliens will hold the same things true and get to grips with what they mean when they speak in those situations. Similarity of belief appears useless for mutual understanding unless we can first pick out the situations in which the beliefs are held. A rejoinder to this could be that the circumstances need only *appear* the same to each of us. The distinction between something being true and its being held true applies here.

We have to identify the situation presumably giving rise to other people's beliefs in order to understand the beliefs. As long as we pick it out in the way it appears to them, we can conclude what they take to be true. It may even be possible sometimes to understand what someone is saying through seeing how circumstances may appear to him, even if we know he is mistaken. The link with truth is completely broken in such a case, although we still need to know what he mistakenly holds true. A replica rabbit running in front of a native will serve as well as a real one for eliciting the word 'gavagai' or some such reaction, if we can be reasonably certain that the native *thinks* it is real. Of course, he will be right that he thinks he sees a rabbit, or that the thing appears to be a rabbit, and we must also believe that this is how things are for him. There must be some overlap between his beliefs and ours. The relevant point is that the overlap does not occur in the beliefs we share about the world. It can exist between his beliefs about what he is seeing and our beliefs about what his beliefs are. The true nature of the world need not enter into it, and, neither, it seems, need there be any similarity of experience. We do not actually have to be experiencing what he is experiencing to form a correct judgement of his experience.

Davidson's requirement that most of our beliefs must be true is far too strong if he merely wishes to obtain an interpretation of an alien language. As long as there is similarity in what is *held* true, there can be contact between our language and that of an alien. Is even this a requirement? Our previous remarks about the possibility of understanding those who hold a belief we know to be mistaken might seem to put this in doubt. There seems no vestige of Davidson's principle of charity left, if we can identify what others hold true even when we do not hold the same things true. It does not seem to matter whether beliefs are true or even whether we share them. This raises the problem whether we could understand the way things appeared to a tribe which was totally mistaken and whose views we did not share at all. It is all very well saying that we can translate *if* we know how they view things even when it is radically different from our way. The difficulty must surely be how we could find out that they viewed things so differently. We are back with the question of the intelligibility of an alternative conceptual scheme. The replica rabbit example was plausible because we could understand how the mistake could easily arise in such a situation. We realize we ourselves would probably make the same error. Understanding what is said when plausible mistakes are made is very much parasitic on normal understanding. Our views about what others probably believe are inevitably formed in the context of what *we* believe. We do not have to assume that different people or tribes will all share largely similar beliefs, but if mistakes occur they have to be intelligible against the background of our beliefs. There are many ways of being mistaken, and once we allow that someone could believe *anything* when confronted with a particular set of circumstances, the possibility of understanding is lost.

Alternative Conceptual Frameworks

The problem of alternative conceptual frameworks is the problem how far people's beliefs can diverge from our own without becoming unintelligible. There has to come a point where we will even wonder whether they have beliefs or whether the noises they make amount to a language. Would a conceptual system be inaccessible to us, if its holders divided the world up differently, noticed differences we ignore and lumped together other things which we think separate? The notion of a world external to conceptual systems becomes crucial at this point. If it is independent of all systems, we may very often be able to see the identifications made by different systems when confronted with the same situation. What makes it the same situation is not dependent on any particular system. Even if one system calls attention, say, to similarities ignored by another, it is still true that the similarities are either actually there or they are not. The activity of combining or distinguishing is distinct from what is combined or distinguished. When we see a cat on a wall we see two things. If some tribe chose for its own reasons to use one word to describe the occurrence and did not even think in terms of two entities, we should be able to find this out. What they see and what we see is the same, even if there might be a sense in which they see one object when we see two. Talk of 'the object' may beg the question at issue between the systems, but there is a situation independent of them and recognized as common to each. Even though the situation will obviously have to be described in terms of one or the other, there is something which must be held true by each. If this seems doubtful, we only have to see how what can reasonably be said *is* constrained by what is there. A system which wanted to hold the equivalent of 'the moon is made of green cheese' or 'water is wet' when confronted with a cat on a wall is obviously so arbitrary and irrational that it will never be understood. There would be no basis for teaching or learning it. We must assume that when people speak when confronted with something, they are talking *about* that thing, even if they wish to view it as a separate entity, part of a larger one, or itself a combination of entities.

One difficulty arising when we want to talk of similarity of belief and yet of possible variations in conceptual systems is that beliefs themselves are conditioned by conceptual systems. The belief that there is a cat on a wall presupposes that the believer thinks of cat and wall as separate entities. The tribe which views it as a single entity will have a different concept. Can we say that any belief is shared when the relevant concepts are not? Undue concentration on concepts and the way in which reality is conceptualized can lead philosophers to think there has to be some neutral way of describing reality, if we are to be able to conceive it as external to all conceptual schemes. It seems as if there has to be some neutral underpinning of them for understanding and translation to occur. I have said that there is an objective situation which *we* would describe as a cat on a wall and others might see as one entity. For us there can be cats not on walls, and walls without cats. We would not be disturbed if *that* cat jumped off *that* wall. The possible tribe we are considering would think an indissoluble unit had gone when the cat left the wall. Presumably they would think something else had come in its place when the wall remained. This is of course very significant. What the tribe says is constrained by what happens. The entity cat-on-wall no longer continues when the cat goes, and their description has to change when ours does. We each respond to what objectively happens and this gives the point of contact between the systems.

The systems each describe the world and respond to its changes. They do not influence the world or determine what happens, except in the sense that they determine how to describe what happens. This itself is no trivial matter, since there is an accurate or inaccurate way of describing things. It is reasonable to ask whether it is more appropriate to think of a cat on a wall as one unit or two. From a biological point of view, it is more satisfactory to distinguish a living creature from an inanimate object, but it is possible to imagine a background of belief where the combination of a cat and wall was infinitely more important to a tribe than each separately. It might be a powerful religious symbol, but in that case the tribe would be ignoring what a biologist thought important.

It is tempting to say that the descriptions which are used to portray reality depend very largely on the needs and interests of a group which may as a result select one thing and ignore another. There is the familiar point that Eskimos are more interested in different types of snow and shades of white than inhabitants of the south of England. If we follow this line of reasoning we will conclude that there may be many equivalent descriptions of reality, and the ones chosen will depend on the frame of reference one is operating in. Reality could be regarded as neutral between these schemes and they could all equally correctly refer to the same reality. What they pick out will vary according to the interests concerned. There is obviously some truth in this. We often do not need to notice differences which may nevertheless be there objectively. Beliefs about the nature of the world may condition our description of it. A mystical belief that the combination of a cat and wall is especially significant could easily influence a tribe's conceptual scheme. How we select depends on prior beliefs and present needs. Yet *what* we select is independent of the process of selection. We might explain the Eskimo's obsession with snow by his environment, but he is either correct about the differences he sees or he is not. They could still be a figment of his imagination. If not, they are accessible to us, and if we lived amongst permanent snow, we would do well to notice them too. We just do not usually need to bother about them. Even the cat-on-wall unit is not an arbitrary combination. Either the tribesman is right in thinking it significant or he is not. His beliefs about its mystical importance depend on religious beliefs which are themselves true or false. If he is right, we should all think it important, and if he is not, it may well be that our distinction between animate and inanimate objects is of far greater importance and that he too would do well to adopt it.

Selection according to interests may explain difference in conceptual schemes, but it is not enough to think that the relativity of interests explain everything. A realist should question the validity of the interests. Even then, though, when interests arising from false belief have been disregarded, there may well be a different form of attention arising from different, but equally valid, sets of interest. One may concentrate on one aspect of reality, the other on another, when both were noticing what is there. For this reason, their separate insights would not be incompatible but could be combined. A race which paid more attention to the firmness or slushiness of snow than to its colour could easily be taught to notice gradations of whiteness, and a race which preferred to pick out differences of colour could easily be led to notice differences in firmness.

An objection may be that even if this is true of some cases, there may well be others where different legitimate interests lead to incompatible divisions of the same part of world. For instance, we may refer to rabbits while one tribe refers to undetached rabbit parts. Assuming it has good reasons for doing so (it might be thinking solely in terms of rabbits as a source of food), we appear to have genuinely alternative divisions of the same piece of reality. Can a fully realist view rest content with this? This is a recurring problem, but it is particularly relevant in considering Davidson. His insistence on the principle of charity stems from his desire to avoid different conceptual systems reflecting the same uninterpreted reality. Yet the notion of alternative conceptual frameworks is only dangerous when reality is no longer thought independent of them. The possibility of correlation between schemes is preserved if it is accepted that there is a dichotomy between concept and thing conceptualized. May we then still be left with two equally good ways of characterizing reality, stemming from interests which are equally valid? There is no problem where, as we have seen, they are drawing attention to different aspects of the same reality.

There is in fact nothing very puzzling about different ways of identifying the same object from different standpoints. Philosophers often remind us that Venus can be picked out both as the Evening Star and as the Morning Star. The star seen in the evening is the same as the one seen in the morning. A realist is not going to start wondering if it is really 'the evening star' or whether 'the morning star' is perhaps a more appropriate description. Venus can be, and is, both. The realist's difficulty is not with this kind of case, but with the possibility of two people at the same place and the same time looking in the same direction and yet making different, and equally valid, distinctions about what is there. Different conceptual systems could then appear to fit equally well on the same reality. Quine's 'gavagai' example is an instance of this, but the indeterminacy is there kept within bounds. The native and the linguist can still talk to each other, since they receive the same sensory stimulation. More radical examples will break any possibility of contact between different ways of seeing the world because they have nothing in common.

Davidson's arguments against a dualism of scheme and content rest on the assumption that reality would be 'waiting to be organized'. In a trivial sense all reality is uninterpreted before we conceptualize it, but this could all too easily carry with it the image of a formless mass, waiting to be shaped. A realist would not accept that we could organize or interpret reality in any way we please. The organization and interpretation made through our conceptual scheme ought to be, if realism is correct, a reflection of the actual structure of the world. We must be wary of concluding that because we can envisage different ways of conceptualizing, all are equally good.

The Definite Character of Reality

Realism cannot accept the picture of the world as a formless mass waiting for some form of organization. It would follow that virtually any organization could be arbitrarily imposed on the inert, passive stuff which is all that nature could be conceived as being. If we assume that nature has a definite structure and that there actually are different entities of the kind science attempts to tell us about, then it follows that a correct conceptual sheme will tell us precisely which ones there are.

The dichotomy between organizing scheme and reality waiting to be organized can itself be given either a realist interpretation or a near-idealist one. The mere admission that there is anything self-subsistent and independent of all conceptual schemes is a concession to realism, but the greater the emphasis on the active and organizing nature of the scheme in comparison with a formless reality, the more pronounced the idealism. A self-subsistent reality has a particular nature whether or not we are able to discover what that is. We have to take a stand on metaphysical questions here. We may wish to agree with Parmenides that reality is a single whole, with no part distinct from any other. If we wish to avoid this paradoxical conclusion, it follows that reality must be composed of entities with different natures and that this is so independently of the conceptual scheme we adopt. The aim of any conceptual system will be to draw the distinctions which already exist in nature. Unless we wish to be conceptual idealists, it is quite wrong to think of nature, reality, things-in-themselves, or however we wish to characterize what there is, as having no definite characteristics before we apply our conceptual system.

This is of major importance in connection with the problem of alternative conceptual systems. The definite character of reality ensures that it provides a very far from neutral basis on which to rest a conceptual scheme. Quine's preoccupation with indeterminacy arose because our experience is not itself sufficient to determine the nature of reality. Once we give up any idea of reducing talk of what there is to talk of our experience, we can move beyond the anthropocentric view of the world and recognize that man's experience does not constitute the world. It is merely the means by which he can come to recognize its independent nature. Experience can give rise to alternative theories, but if we realize that theories are *about* something, then either reality is as the theory says or it is not. It has a determinate character, even if we do not know what it is. This is a metaphysical assertion, but it expresses the only alternative to the view that all is in fact indeterminate chaos, a view which would make the practice of science a pointless activity. As a result, alternative conceptual systems cannot be accepted as all resting *correctly* on the same base in reality. Unless they can be combined in some way, and are not genuine alternatives, they are disagreeing about the actual characteristics of reality. They all assert that reality has a definite nature and differ as to what it is. The essence of realism is that there is a right and a wrong in such a situation. Realism is committed to a two-valued logic. Either reality is as a theory or system says it is or it is not.

The notion of alternative conceptual systems is not incoherent, even when they are genuine alternatives. It is mistaken to imagine that the only choice is understanding a language from the standpoint of our own or denying it is a genuine language. The world provides the standard with which to judge languages. The view that if there are different conceptual systems they are all equally good can only stem from a metaphysical assumption about the nature of reality. Being mistaken may be a matter of degree, but the most adequate system in principle will be the one which properly reflects natural distinctions. We cannot, as Davidson would wish to do, simply rule out the possibility of different and incompatible descriptions of the same piece of reality. The mere fact of alternative conceptual systems need not lead to conceptual relativism (assuming that we mean by this more than that it is possible to have different systems). One system can easily be more successful in the portrayal of reality than another. Some may be just plain wrong.

We may be accused here, as realists customarily are, of a massive begging of the question. We are not, though, assuming that reality is merely 'reality-for-us', and that the world is in fact just as we conceive it. Only a realist interpretation can give proper weight to the possibility of error. One consequence is that *our* conceptual system may be mistaken in some fundamental way. It is in this respect that Davidson's view that most of our beliefs must be correct seems exceedingly curious. We not only safeguard ourselves against any fundamental scepticism, if we take his statement seriously, but we also remove the urge for constant criticism of our beliefs and for the continuous quest for new knowledge. He was no doubt thinking of straightforward empirical beliefs, and it would indeed be difficult to start questioning seriously whether the sun is shining or whether we see a cat on the wall, given optimum viewing conditions. The assumption that we all for the most part experience the same world in the same way is indeed a precondition for mutual comprehension. Davidson's requirement emphasizes the need for a point of contact between alternative schemes. This need not take the form of demanding that different schemes overlap so much that in the end we can safely rule out the possibility of a radically different scheme. An appeal to an objective world can provide the necessary common factor. Indeed Davidson's rhetoric is hard to take very seriously. How could we ever decide if most of our or other people's beliefs were true? What counts as a belief anyway? There are many areas, more complicated than mere observational situations, where one does not need to be unduly cynical to think that most beliefs are false. It does not seem self-contradictory to think that in the course of human history, most people's moral and political beliefs have been false. It would seem the height of parochialism to respond that if the beliefs are different from ours, they cannot be identified as 'moral' or 'political'.

Davidson's flat earth example suggests that he means to apply his view consistently even to apparently compromising examples. Yet the principle of charity, which impels us to look for reason and truth in what others say, can be far too charitable. We must take the fact of human error seriously, and of course allow for our own possible error. Nevertheless this is not a lapse into scepticism, since the fact that we may be mistaken does not mean we can never be right. Truth is attainable, because reality is accessible. Davidson's example, however, raises the question how we can be sure that someone with a large number of false beliefs about an entity *is* referring to that entity and not something else. There must come a point where we may wish to deny he is talking of *that*, although a crude enumeration of beliefs does not seem to be the way we would decide. Any number of mistaken scientific beliefs about the earth would not tend to undermine our acceptance that this earth is being referred to in the flat earth case. The ancients were talking about the earth they were living on and could have defined it ostensively. We could see what they were intending to pick out by means of this one correct belief. It would be irrelevant if we discovered over half their beliefs were wrong, assuming we knew how to count them. Someone's intentions in referring seem much more relevant in asking what he is referring to than any question about mistaken beliefs.

When we see that *what* terms refer to is independent of the way they are picked out, we will accept that what is referred to by a term cannot be identified with any particular description. Descriptions can vary from time to time as knowledge progresses, but an object picked out at one time by one theory may be the same as an object picked out rather differently in a subsequent version of the theory, or even a new theory altogether. Something on the lines of the principle of charity invoked by Davidson has been used by Putnam[7] to cover this kind of case. He prefers to call it the 'principle of benefit of the doubt'. Instead of assuming that most people's beliefs must be true, he appeals to what people would have said given our knowledge, rather than theirs, in order to determine whether we and they are talking about the same things. If they specified something by means of a description relying on a mistaken belief, he says that 'we should assume that they would accept reasonable reformulations of their descriptions'. He gives the example of Bohr's reference to electrons in the early 1900s. Bohr continued to talk of 'electrons' even though he modified his views and introduced the concept of complementarity. In this case, he came himself to the conclusion that he had earlier been mistaken, but he thought that his later views were still about the entities he had been intending to refer to thirty years before. He accepted that if he had known in 1904 what he knew in 1934, he would have used 'electron' then to refer to what his later knowledge indicated.

It is not always as simple, and it is sometimes left to a later generation to modify the views of an earlier one. If, though, it is reasonable to suppose that, given the later knowledge the earlier generation would itself have modified its views about some particular thing, both could quite easily be understood to be referring to the same object. The intentions of both were the same. One was more successful than the other in putting them into practice. We can obviously expect some attempts at identification to be better than others, if objects exist independently of the means by which they are picked out. Poor attempts, however, do not necessarily fail to refer. Reference is not an all or nothing affair, whereby we have the choice of being right about an object or of not referring at all. Theories can give mistaken descriptions and yet these descriptions can still be of something. Otherwise the notion of mistake would be totally irrelevant, because there would be nothing to be mistaken about.

If we accept that someone really meant to refer to the same

entities we wish to talk about, he must have had *some* approximately correct beliefs about them. We must be careful not to read too much into what people have said. The principle of the benefit of the doubt could degenerate into the truism that if anyone had known what we know now, they would have referred to what we do. There must be some indication that they were trying to refer to the same things we refer to. It would not be very illuminating to foist the concept of an electron on to the early Greek scientists. Presumably they would not have held the views they did if they knew what we know about the atom. As it was, they thought that atoms were indivisible and so could not possibly have had the concept of an electron. They did not intend to refer to anything sub-atomic. Bohr's earlier views, on the other hand, were concerned with particles and there are particles which approximately fit his description. It is reasonable to suppose he meant to refer to them. His earlier theory differed from his later one, but they can both be understood to be about the same entities.

Returning to the flat earth case, there can be no doubt what the ancients intended to refer to, even given their mistaken beliefs. They were referring to the earth we inhabit, and they were wrong in what they said. Davidson runs the risk of denying there can ever be substantial disagreement, with his view that apparent disagreement puts in question the correctness of interpretation. Whatever the difficulties of having to identify beliefs while meanings are in doubt and vice versa, it is no solution to deny the difference by insisting on a methodological assumption on the similarity of beliefs. Any theory which makes fundamental disagreement impossible, whether within a language or between languages, ignores one of the most basic facts of life.

Davidson repudiates the idea that any *thing* makes sentences or theories true. He says:[8] 'Not experience, not surface irritations, not the world, can make a sentence true. . . The sentence 'My skin is warm' is true if and only if my skin is warm. Here there is no reference to a fact, a world, an experience, or a piece of evidence.'

Davidson is here using Tarski's test for theories of truth. That provides a list into which all the sentences go which are capable of being formed in a language L of given syntax. For each sentence, true or false, there is a statement of the conditions under which it is true. There is, however, nothing in Tarski's work to justify what Davidson says. 'My skin is warm' is certainly true in English if and only if my skin is warm, but the question remains what makes it true that my skin is warm. Being told what sentences the concept of truth may be applied to does not help with the fundamental problem why these sentences, rather than others, can be regarded as true. Davidson remarks that 'we recognize sentences like " 'snow is white' is true if and only if snow is white" to be trivially true'. He goes on to point out that nevertheless 'the totality of such English sentences uniquely determines the concept of truth for English'. Yet what we now want is a way of saying what all the *true* sentences, out of the Tarski list of all sentences, have in common. Davidson so concentrates on truth as a property of sentences in a language that he is in danger of underrating the role of the things which languages describe. He would, of course, agree that 'snow is white' is about white snow, but his emphasis on the importance of translatability ensures that he concentrates on lignuistic properties to the virtual exclusion of any notion of extra-linguistic reality. Indeed, although he is not denying the reality of the world in any way, he would no doubt think of the distinctions drawn by words such as 'white' or 'snow' in purely linguistic terms. Since these distinctions can only be made by language, it is easy to see the temptation of not going beyond it. Yet the reason we can expect to understand other languages, even if they express alien conceptual schemes, is not because we all share the same true beliefs, but because we are attempting to talk about a world common to us all.

Reality and Concepts

It might appear tempting to say that mind and reality fit each other, so that reality is what in principle can be conceived by mind. If we go further and relate mind to linguistic capacity, we will conclude that language and reality fit each other. Reality is then what can in principle be expressed in language. The investigation of language then becomes a substitute for metaphysics, and reality is made highly anthropocentric. The distinctions drawn by language are considered real enough in the world, simply because the world *is* what is described in language. This limitation of what is the case to what can be talked about entails there is nothing beyond the scope of language, and thus is a metaphysical conclusion about the nature of reality.

What cannot be talked about cannot be talked about, so it would be self-defeating to give examples, but it is not obviously self-evident to say that what cannot be talked about does not exist. Any preoccupation with language inevitably tends to this conclusion. If we hold that what cannot be approximately translated into English cannot be classified as language, and combine this with the metaphysical assumption about the close relationship of reality to linguistic possibilities, we will conclude that the nature of reality is limited to the capabilities of the English language. This seems an extraordinarily parochial position. Language develops, and indeed there is an analogy with scientific progress. It would still be rash to say that reality is what science will one day describe. Peirce's 'final opinion' is an elusive concept, unless it collapses into the realist position that reality is in principle accessible to science. Since, though, this 'in principle' usually refers to logical possibility, it often cloaks a physical impossibility. It sometimes appears to be saying that it is logically possible for physical science to do what is physically impossible. This is hardly helpful, since it would be a denial of the nature of physical science to be free of physical impossibility.

Reference to what is in principle expressible in language is similarly misleading. It is not really saying anything about language at all if it is only talking of what it is logically possible to speak about. 'What is in principle expressible' is being used as a synonym for 'what exists'. No effort is being made to examine the actual potentialities of language, or the limitations of language-users. The latter are particularly relevant, since human language cannot actually be used in connection with anything entirely beyond the reach of humans. Saying that some state of affairs, perhaps at the other end of the universe, which will forever be beyond our reach, is expressible in human language is hardly helpful. The assertion relies on a realist view for any plausibility it may have. Unless we first assume there *are* things beyond our reach, we cannot say that it is logically possible to talk of them even though we know we never will. If we seriously want to restrict ourselves to the actual capabilities of a natural language, we have to start there and make reality conform to it rather than try to do the opposite. Such a position implicitly asserts that snow is white because we say it is, and indeed that 'it' is snow because we say so. However imprecise and approximate the concepts concerned may be, the reverse is the case. We say that snow is white, because that is how things are. Reality is not necessarily fitted to language, but we try to make our language fit reality.

'Start from where you are' is a very seductive doctrine, and references to 'inexpressible reality' always invite accusations that the Kantian thing-in-itself is being reintroduced into the scheme of things. R. Rorty has presented the dilemma succinctly. He says that the notion of 'the world' used in phrases such as 'different conceptual schemes carve up the world differently', must be of something completely unspecified and unspecifiable. He continues:[9] 'I want to claim that "the world" is either the purely vacuous notion of the ineffable cause of sense and goal of intellect, or else a name for the objects that inquiry at the moment is leaving alone.'

In other words, we must adopt a purely pragmatic notion of the world or make it so inaccessible that it serves no genuine purpose. Rorty holds that once we have started thinking of 'the world' as made up of anything in particular, whether atoms and void, sense data, Quine's surface stimulations or anything else, 'we are', he says, 'now well within some particular theory about how the world is'. He considers that ' "truth" in the sense of "truth taken apart from any theory" and "world" taken as "what determines such truth" are notions that were made for each other'. He believes that neither can survive without the other. Yet we must be wary of thinking that truth must be viewed apart from all theories, if it is to be linked with 'world'. Rorty has fallen into the trap of thinking that if truth has links with 'the world', it must be totally detached from all theories, or itself become merely a notion within a theory. Since what the world is cannot itself be a matter for theory, we are left, he thinks, with having to make it something totally inaccessible and ineffable. We are presented with the stark choice of making the nature of the world a matter of mere theory, or of preserving its objectivity by making it inaccessible.

We have met this dilemma before, and our answer to it should now be clear. It is a false choice. Different conceptual schemes may indeed carve up 'the world' differently and 'the world' is outside all such schemes, but this does not mean it is an inaccessible something of which we can know nothing. All the schemes do have access to it. Some may be more successful than others in capturing the nature of reality, but they cannot be seen in isolation from their attempts to describe it. Reality may be independent of all schemes, but they do not appear in a vacuum. They are produced by people who are trying to put into conceptual form the nature of that reality, and the best scheme will come closest to showing reality as it is. There is then a middle course between conceptual idealism and the Kantian belief in things-in-themselves.

Are we then to take over Peirce's notion of a final opinion, putting it perhaps in a philosophical rather than a specifically scientific context? Can we say with one philosopher[10] that 'the world may have a conceptualizable structure because there is *some* conceptual scheme or other that is adequate to it'? Yet we may well wonder what could be meant by saying that *some* conceptual scheme is adequate for describing the world. We have agreed that the world can be conceptualized and is not forever lurking beyond all conceptual schemes. The question remains whether we are to say that an absolutely correct conceptual scheme will, or even can, be arrived at. The conceptual millennium seems as unlikely as Peirce's scientific one. We should have to ignore human limitations if *the* final conceptual scheme is to be regarded as in some way mirroring reality. Yet once we do that, the whole idea of a conceptual scheme becomes very foggy. What could it be, if it might never be possessed and used by man?

It is far too optimistic to think that 'the world' could ever be wholly conceptualized by man. It might be 'in principle', but this is merely to say that if men were, for instance, in the right place at the right time they would be able to obtain a concept of such-and-such. The idea of such a concept is not very relevant if it is physically impossible for men ever to be there or to send instruments instead. No doubt everything would lie within men's conceptual grasp if they were omniscient, but a conceptual scheme which had to rely on omniscience to gain currency is hardly a live option. Reference to it at first sight seems to involve little more than saying there is something for it to be about, and we are back with realism.

The view that all 'the world' or 'the universe' can be conceptualized does say more than that the world is there, since it is committed to holding that the world has a particular kind of structure. The world must, for instance, be sufficiently stable to allow for the reidentification of objects after an interval. An objective world would defy any attempted systematization if it were sufficiently chaotic and fluid. Yet some philosophers have precisely this image of the world. They think in terms of concepts stamping some kind of order on the world. Since this is obviously not any kind of causal process, with the conceptual scheme having an actual effect on the world, they must concede that we merely see an

actually chaotic world *as if* it were ordered. This begs the
question how concepts are acquired and passed on. Without a
stable object to which we can draw other people's attention
and which we can point out again subsequently, we would
not be able to get them to understand what we are referring
to. The objectivity of the distinctions we wish to make,
together with a normal similarity in individuals' perception
of them, is indispensable for our ability to communicate with
each other at the level of ordinary empirical concerns. Many
forms of idealism can never satisfactorily explain the public
character of language and of the concepts encapsulated in it,
because they regard the divisions and distinctions we wish to
make in the world as projections from the human mind. Each
person's mind can, of course, make the same projections, but
it seems a miracle that they always happen to do so on the
same occasions. We may also wonder what, without an
objective world, could count as 'the same occasion'.

The view that the world can be conceptualized has to take
account of the abilities of those operating with the concepts.
It is logically possible that there be a concept of *anything*
which exists, but human limitations ensure that reality and
what is covered by men's concepts will not be coextensive.
Some things are inaccessible, sometimes because they are
unobservable, and theories can still refer to them. Other
entities may remain totally beyond understanding. Yet
inaccessibility is not a logical matter. 'Things-in-themselves'
or 'substances' are always just beyond the reach of man,
because it is a logical truth that they lie behind all appearances. The choice is *not* between things-in-themselves or
things-for-us. We can have concepts of things *as* they exist in
themselves. Entities lying beyond the grasp of one generation may well become accessible to a later one, by means of
ever more powerful microscopes and telescopes. The
theoretical entities of one stage of science can become the
observed entities of another. Some entities may be more
inaccessible than others. Yet man's inability to come to grips
with them is an empirical matter.

How far is reality related to our present beliefs about what is real? This is just asking whether our beliefs are true. There is no automatic connection between truth and what we happen to believe. The point of believing anything is certainly that we hope it is true. Truth is our goal, but it is another matter whether we have reached it. We cannot take the easy way out and make it a matter of definition that we have, even in a majority of cases. Although truth may be a semantic notion, it is indissolubly linked with what makes a sentence true. We cannot artificially close the gap between our beliefs and what they are about, no matter how great our fear of scepticism. Wholesale scepticism is probably a self-defeating position, but a certain humility about how much we actually do know may be no bad thing. The dualism of concepts and reality is inescapable. Like the cynic's view of love and marriage, it is possible to have one without the other.

5 THE SOCIOLOGY OF KNOWLEDGE

Sociology of Knowledge or Sociology of Belief?

A certain scepticism about the accessibility of reality and hence the intelligibility of the notion inevitably leads away from questions concerning the connections between truth and reality to a consideration of what men hold true. It is easy to think that beliefs which very often seem to vary so markedly do so because of differences in the background of those holding them. When two men are presented with what are apparently the same facts and come to different conclusions, it is natural to conclude that the explanation lies with the men rather than the purported facts. Disputes will then be explained psychologically or sociologically. It seems very tempting to explain error like this, and show how some people can be so mistaken. Yet this raises the question why we should not also explain the fact that some people are apparently correct by elements in their individual or social background. Some then find it attractive to turn to the psychologist or sociologist for an explanation of *true* belief.

This happens particularly in the so-called 'sociology of knowledge', some versions of which strike at the very roots of traditional views about the role of epistemology in opening up a path to reality. As always, this kind of denial of 'objective reality' can be self-contradictory, since it would be very easy for a sociologist of knowledge to assume that the causal explanations he is offering have themselves some kind of objective validity. To be consistent, he must recognize that sociological explanations are as much the product of social conditioning as any other kind of explanation or belief. The practice of the sociology of knowledge is itself a fit object of study for sociologists. The snag is that an infinite regress can be generated in this way. A sociologist will at no stage be able to say something with a claim to truth if the assumptions behind the sociology of knowledge are justified. It will always only be what he and his colleagues believe, and some other sociologist could easily show how their beliefs were socially conditioned.

The 'sociology of knowledge' is a curious title. It is a philosophical commonplace that knowledge implies the truth of what is known and that I cannot know what is false. Thus it looks as if we have to know what is true before we can engage in the sociology of knowledge. We cannot otherwise know what can count as knowledge. It is a sad fact that a lot of purported knowledge is not knowledge at all, but merely false belief. This is not a terminological quibble, and very often the sociology of knowledge has adopted that title because it has already taken up a certain view of the nature of knowledge and truth. A realist conception of knowledge, which claimed that all knowledge was based on how things actually are, would limit the scope of the sociologist. Indeed there could not be very much left for him to do in this area if it were accepted that the source of knowledge lay in reality rather than in particular social circumstances. Only the view that society largely or wholly conditions our beliefs can provide work for the sociology of knowledge.

Some recent writers have explicitly put the question of truth on one side, and have made the sociology of knowledge one of belief. Even then its scope will be settled by how far beliefs are thought to be influenced by factors other than what the beliefs are about. Nevertheless whatever passes for 'knowledge' in a particular area is accepted as subject matter, and this embraces a wide range. Those[1] influenced by phenomenology think that questions of truth can be 'bracketed off', and that 'knowledge' can be treated as a phenomenon detached from any links with the world. They think that the task of sociology is to investigate the processes by which what passes for knowledge in society is transmitted in social situations. This is a legitimate exercise as long as it is borne in mind that what a society takes to be knowledge may not be knowledge, any more than what is held true may be true.

Is the term 'sociology of knowledge' just an unfortunate misnomer? We could recognize that its subject matter is 'knowledge' and not knowledge, what is taken to be knowledge rather than what is knowledge. Even then there could be problems, since a deterministic sociology of belief could not simply leave the question of truth untouched. There is no reason why a sociologist of knowledge should be a determinist and the sociology of knowledge could be very similar to the history of ideas, so that the ideas studied may or may not be justified. Yet the discipline is much less ambitious when it eschews determinism, since it can no longer hope to find a complete explanation for the holding or transmission of belief. It is left with accounting for possible social influences even though they can be rationally resisted. Determinism gives a major role to the discipline, especially when social pressures are taken to be amongst the most prevalent causes of belief and behaviour.

Many practitioners of the sociology of knowledge would not think in terms of a gentlemanly investigation into possible social influences but would make much wider claims for the discipline. J. Habermas, for example, notes that we very often deceive ourselves about the true motives of our actions, and call it rationalization, while on the level of collective actions, it is called ideology. He says:[2] 'Against the uncontrolled influence of deeper interests, characteristic not so much of individuals as of the objective situation of social groups, a new discipline has even come into existence, the sociology of knowledge.'

Habermas conceives of the discipline as having a therapeutic effect. Its function is to show the real interests governing the beliefs of a society, in the same way as a psychoanalyst might uncover the real motives for the actions of an individual. It demonstrates the social basis for such beliefs and proves that they are held for different reasons than are admitted by those who share them.

The view that the sociology of knowledge should unmask ideology implies that its practitioners are sure they themselves possess knowledge and can distinguish between what is ideological and what is not. They should be able to explain why they are able to see what is really so and are not subject to distorting influences. It is hardly surprising that some other sociologists of knowledge take things to their logical conclusion and accept that everything is ideological and that *no-one* can shake himself sufficiently free of his background to approach reality.

One way in which the sociology of knowledge might lay claim to some importance from an epistemological standpoint is by the assumption that investigating the origins of belief is relevant in some way to questions about its truth. In that case, it looks as if we would have to deny the so-called 'genetic fallacy', according to which historical and social origins of beliefs have to be separated from questions concerning justification. The fallacy is held to lie in confusing questions of origin with questions about validity and truth, but if origins and truth were linked the sociology of knowledge would help us in our search for truth by its investigation into origins.

One example of a theory linking origins to truth in a social context is that of Lukacs. His view was that the proletariat's social and historical position enables and in fact compels it to see the whole of society as it really is. He says:[3] 'It was necessary for the proletariat to be born for social reality to become fully conscious. The reason for this is that the discovery of the class outlook of the proletariat provided a vantage point from which to survey the whole of society.' For Lukacs,[4] 'the self-understanding of the proletariat is simultaneously the objective understanding of the nature of society'. Social and economic factors produce knowledge for the proletariat, while they stop the bourgeoisie from seeing the true nature of society. In each case the origin of the belief, rather than what is believed, is crucial.

Lukacs make the judgement that the proletariat has been put in a position of knowledge about society by a process of social and economic causation. We may well wonder how *he* knows what constitutes knowledge, and he certainly needs some independent criterion with which to judge that these causal factors lead to knowledge. Yet if he has one, this merely serves to demonstrate how knowledge and truth are not tied to particular origins but are accessible to reason. It seems impossible to conclude where the truth lies without some such criteria and some assurance that reality, whether social or any other kind, is accessible. The proletariat may have been placed by capitalism in a peculiarly good vantage point for judging the whole of society, but it seems impossible to say whether this is so without prior knowledge of the nature of society. Indeed, Lukacs' own views can be regarded as the reflection of his social and economic circumstances, if we accept the framework of economic determinism in which he appears to work. There seems no way, given that this is so, of deciding whether Lukacs is right and he has been caused to believe correctly that the proletariat have been caused to have correct beliefs. Who can say?

Criticisms like this rest on the assumption that the source of truth lies in objective reality and that a sharp distinction can be drawn between a belief and its truth, because what makes a belief true is totally independent of the fact of its being held. It follows that the cause or origin of belief is only relevant if it provides a path to reality. Lukacs not surprisingly holds views on the nature of truth and reality which are markedly different. He is primarily concerned with social reality, but his views have wider implications. He seizes on Heraclitus' doctrine of flux according to which there is no stable reality. Nothing is; everything 'becomes', or is in process. He considers[5] indeed that Heraclitus did not go far enough, since the eternal flux itself seems to be fixed. It is, and does not itself become. Lukacs advocates instead the Marxian dialectical process 'where the objective forms of the objects are themselves transformed into a process, a flux'. He says: 'The knowledge that social facts are not objects but relations between men is intensified to the point where facts are wholly dissolved into processes.'

Since reality is in flux and objects are transformed into processes, the emphasis shifts from the discovery and understanding of an independent reality to a more active involvement with processes. Nothing in society is fixed. 'Man', according to Lukacs, 'has become the measure of all (societal) things'. We are told that reality must be understood concretely as a historical process. Theory and practice must be united and it then becomes possible to change reality.

The union of theory and practice, and the involvement of men in concrete historical processes, provide a very different kind of picture from that of men trying to understand a reality with a distinct existence. Truth is then created rather than discovered, although the nature of reality is not made to depend on thought in any idealist sense. Lukacs considers the dichotomy between thought and reality a false one. Reality cannot reflect thought, because, according to Lukacs, it is wrong to separate the two and then look for a correspondence between them. They are instead both aspects of the same historical process.

It is regarded as a virtue by positions like this that the distinction between the subject and object of knowledge is abolished, with the result that reality can never be understood to be self-subsistent. Men possess knowledge, and men are primary. The influences on them then become of paramount importance, and what men know becomes subordinated to how they know. This view arises a result of the decision to treat the movements of history as the true reality. The fact of a change in belief is then much more important than any question about whether a belief is true. Such a question becomes nonsensical after the abolition of the notion of a reality to which consciousness tries to conform. Thought is merely part of the total process.

The sociology of knowledge becomes especially important once the concepts of truth and reality are subordinated in this way. Any *a priori* approach to the possibility of knowledge is impossible with the overthrow of the distinction between theory and practice. Karl Mannheim made the sociology of knowledge superior to epistemology and held the following:[6] 'The function of the findings of the sociology of knowledge lies somewhere in a fashion hitherto not clearly understood between irrelevance to the establishment of truth on the one hand and entire adequacy for determining truth on the other.'

He realized that this meant he was committing the genetic fallacy, and was quite happy to revise the thesis that, as he put it, 'the genesis of a proposition is under all circumstances irrelevant to its truth'. He believed that truth and origin were closely linked, but once again, it proved impossible to hold this kind of theory while keeping to a traditional view of truth. Mannheim believed it is a function of sociology to relate intellectual phenomena to the perspective of a given situation and as a result to determine the extent of their validity. Despite what he says, this merely seems a form of relativism. He admits 'that in this relational process one does not merely relate the assertion to a standpoint but, in doing so, restricts its claim to validity which at first was absolute, to a narrower scope'. He is in fact denying the whole possibility of any form of objective truth. Like Lukacs, he is opposed[7] to the 'static world view of intellectualism' and is attracted by the notion of 'a realm in which everything is in the process of becoming'. He says:[8]

> The ideal of a realm of truth as such (which so to speak pre-exists independently of the historical-psychological act of thought, and in which every concrete act of knowing merely participates) is the last off-shoot of the dualistic world view which alongside of our world of concrete, immediate events, created a second world by adding another dimension of being.

Instead, Mannheim wants to make truth depend on what people think. He grudgingly admits that the notion of 'truth in itself' has some 'heuristic value for such modes of thought as are represented by the example $2 \times 2 = 4$'. On the whole, however, he thinks that we should realize that knowing is the act of a living being, and that we should use the sociology of knowledge to examine the various influences on thought.

The Sociology of Science

An excessive emphasis on social conditioning at the expense of any idea of the pursuit of truth has repercussions for education. One writer remarks:[9] 'The problems which are thought to reside in a "body" of knowledge and the rules for their effective solution or verification are themselves socially constructed.' What counts as 'knowledge' or 'truth' is thus a reflection of the pressures of society, and consequently, teaching can no longer be understood as the imparting of truth. Indeed he defines education by saying: 'We shall conceptualize teaching and learning as the intersubjective construction of reality.' This particular application of the sociology of knowledge illustrates how the discipline persistently shifts attention from the content of belief to actual men believing.

When it is applied to science and the activity of scientists, the problems are seen in their starkest form. Issues may not seem as clear-cut in the context of beliefs about the nature of society. Societies are made by man. Although social pressures can and do exist independently of people's awareness of them, and this gives rise to the possibility of *false* consciousness, the pressures are obviously not independent of man as such. When we investigate science from a sociological point of view, things are much clearer. The principle may not be different, but the consequences of abandoning realism are even more radical. Scientists investigate what we loosely call 'nature'. Yet what can its status be, when all the scientific theories about it are merely the result of influences which have nothing to do with it? One retort may be that even the realist must accept that scientists are not always as rational as they might be. However, it is one thing to say that scientists can be influenced by irrelevant considerations and quite another to hold that there is no such distinction between 'relevant' and 'irrelevant'. We would then be faced with scientists and their beliefs, with no access to any reality to enable us to check which beliefs are held because of factors unconnected with it.

A parallel argument has to be faced by sociologists of knowledge themselves. Treatment, for instance, of the various causes influencing scientists can easily rest on the assumption that these causes are waiting to be discovered. This is a realist view and a consistent sociologist of knowledge has to recognize that he cannot simply be talking of objective causal relationships, even if he merely thinks of causation in terms of constant conjunctions (which would still be objectively there). He can only express his own socially conditioned beliefs. When science is regarded as a fit object of study for sociology, social science must be as well. The sociologist has to accept that he *never* has access to any reality, but only has beliefs, which may be the result of his own sociological work, and may equally well be the outcome of his position in society.

Sociologists of knowledge are forever impaled on a dilemma. They can have an ambitious view of the scope of their subject, but must then apply it to their own discipline. This will make it much less significant for other people, since there seems no compelling reason why they should accept what are merely the socially conditioned prejudices of others. On the other hand, a sociologist of knowledge might concede that access to various forms of reality is possible and that we can escape our prejudices and social pressure on us. He can then consistently claim truth for his own findings, but does so at a cost. His subject has to be restricted, since social pressure or any other kind of causation, is not wholly explanatory if rational consideration of evidence is possible. He must accept that scientists *can* consider findings arrived at by their method in a dispassionate way. In that case, the sociology of science, as a species of the sociology of knowledge, can only hope to reach some broad generalizations. Epistemology must once again become a force with which to reckon. The sociology of knowledge is, therefore, either nihilistic in a self-defeating way, or it is harmless and of little epistemological importance.

Many of the practitioners of the sociology of science wish to abolish any distinctions between judgements made on the evidence and those swayed by other factors. They claim that the 'genetic fallacy' is no fallacy at all. One historian of science writes:[10]

> The traditional distinction between genetic and analytic accounts in philosophy and science should be softened so as to mesh in with the weaker use of that distinction in interpersonal and social interpretations. Similarly the whole distinction between the content and validity of an idea and its context should also be considerably softened. Nothing is ultimately contextual: all is constitutive.

The writer acknowledges that objective nature exists but he claims that 'all attempts to know it—to qualify or quantify it in any way—are inescapably mediated through human consciousness, and consciousness is a socio-political and ideological mediator'.

This kind of position has many links with idealism, with its emphasis on consciousness. Starting with consciousness rather than reality inevitably leads to worry about the accessibility of reality, since there seems no way of deciding whether our consciousness is of reality or whether it has been deflected in any way. The very problem must be dismissed as nonsensical. Even if it is accepted that 'nature' or 'reality' is objective, its character is forever beyond our grasp. We may have beliefs about it, but these may have been formed for reasons which have nothing to do with what its character actually is. Such an approach must make it tempting to scrap the whole notion of objective reality, and accept instead that our concepts of reality and nature are as socially conditioned as political concepts are alleged to be. Lukacs[11] himself said that nature is a 'social category'. Beliefs about reality must be regarded on this view as mere reflections of the prevailing ideology. Human consciousness then appears to be what matters, together with the many factors which go to make that up. The job of the sociology of knowledge appears to be to unravel them.

An insistence on the 'genetic fallacy' must curtail the ambitions of the sociology of knowledge. It is essential that the fallacy be recognized as such, as long as we maintain a realist position. The possibility of false belief indicates that some causes can lead people away from reality, and in that instance what makes someone believe something is obviously different from what makes that belief true. The interference of an extraneous factor can often explain the error. Special interests may be at work predisposing the holder of a belief to a wrong interpretation of the facts. The sociology of knowledge can be attractive when it explains the advent of false beliefs. Sometimes all the relevant evidence may not be available, and ignorance itself is at times an adequate explanation of error. Yet often two people or two societies can come to different conclusions when apparently faced with exactly the same evidence, and it is tempting to think that there may be psychological or sociological reasons why different insights should be given to the same thing. Since the explanation cannot lie in the evidence, an 'external' factor appears to have intervened. A particular social background for instance, may produce a predisposition to favour certain types of evidence while ignoring others.

Talking of 'external' rather than 'internal' factors seems easy enough, but fierce debates rage in the philosophy of science as to what precisely the distinction is. This problem is interwoven with the argument about the genetic fallacy. The causes of belief which are held to be irrelevant to questions of truth are precisely the external factors which are contrasted with internal ones. In other words, 'internal' grounds for belief seem to be those related to questions of truth, whereas 'external' factors in producing belief are those which do not contribute to the truth conditions of what we believe. To take an everyday example, when I believe it is raining because I hear the rain driving against the window, the noise of the rain is part of what justifies us in saying it is raining. It is an internal factor. On the other hand, if my belief is induced by a drug, the administration of the drug could occur whether it is raining or not. It can have nothing to do with whether it is raining and is therefore an 'external' factor.

We may very well be unaware of external influences on us, and the sociologist of knowledge thinks it his function to reveal them when grounded in the structure of a society. Being conscious of them does not make them 'internal' in any way, although we may then be in a position to resist them to some extent. External factors are not reasons for believing which turn out to be bad ones because they mislead us. The difference between bad reasons and what is no reason at all is important. External factors are not even starters as reasons. They can explain how a belief was acquired, but they do not purport to justify or support its content in any way. The ground of a belief is the evidence we think we have for its truth. We may sometimes be mistaken about whether it really is evidence, or we may give too much weight to evidence which is not in fact very strong. Our belief will in those cases be false. Nevertheless for the belief to be rational, we must think there is a connection between our grounds and what is the case. The grounds of belief may be bad but causes, merely in so far as they are causes, cannot furnish us with reasons at all. What is a cause may also be a reason, but that does not mean that causes *as such* are reasons.

Saying that internal factors in belief are those related to the truth of the belief is far too strong, because we have to allow for the possibility that the belief is false. We must say that they are thought to be related to the truth of the belief. They would be the kind of thing produced as a reason for belief by the holder of the belief, and would be thought directly related to the content of the belief. This marks a significant contrast between the internal and the external. So-called 'external' factors are only accidentally related to the content. They can explain why a belief is held at a particular time, but they explain the *fact* of belief and are not primarily concerned with *what* is believed. The emphasis is on why a belief is held rather than on the merits of its content.

Sociology's Challenge to the Authority of Science

It is tempting to expect sociology to explain the existence of error at a particular time. Sociology always looks at men with beliefs rather than simply at what is believed. It is more concerned with the fact of the holding of a belief at a particular time than with abstract questions of truth and rationality. It looks at actual men in actual social settings. Once, though, the precedent of explaining the fact of belief is followed, it might seem difficult to apply it merely to false belief, and the way is open for the sociology of knowledge. R. K. Merton[12] comments that 'the sociology of knowledge came into being with the signal hypothesis, that even truths were to be held socially accountable'. That marks a decisive step away from the view that arriving at the truth is self-explanatory while deviations from it have to be explained.

This is all particularly relevant in studying the development of science. Why were scientists of earlier times so mistaken? They very often did not have the necessary equipment for observation and experiment and as a result had insufficient or misleading data on which to base their theories. This kind of explanation is one about the origins of ignorance and error. Sociologists of science are more and more frequently posing the question why we should want a causal explanation of error and yet feel that scientific discovery and progress needs no such explanation. One writer says:[13]

> Sociological causation should not be invoked to explain beliefs simply because they are apparently erroneous or irrational. In practice, this means that causal (and functional) accounts of beliefs have fre-

quently been unsoundly based through sociology as a whole. As critics have frequently pointed out, causal sociological analyses have, in effect, been parochial and evaluative. They have justified the beliefs of the sociologist and those he most esteems in his own society, and explained away the conceptions of others as distortions. Social scientists have lacked any real curiosity about the status of their own beliefs.

The same writer continues by saying that sociological work has been misconceived not because it has employed such explanations, but because 'it has wrongly identified the baseline from which such explanations must operate, and has not recognized the need to subject *all* beliefs and practices to them'. In other words, causal explanations should not just be used to account for deviations from the path of rationality and of truth, but should account for the holding of *all* beliefs, including those scientific beliefs we judge correct. Natural science is no longer treated as the exemplar of that dispassionate search for truth which will inevitably reach its goal unless diverted by external considerations. It merely becomes a body of belief which is no better and no worse than other systems of belief. Barnes says:[14]

> Science enjoys no advantage because its beliefs are in unique correspondence with reality or uniquely rational; hence its process of cultural transmission will be in no important respect different to those employed by other knowledge sources. Like the prophet, the astrologer, and the witch-doctor, the teacher of science will have to deal with the problem of his own credibility: he is faced with the task of transmitting lore.

It is hardly surprising that science is put in such company, since any preoccupation with belief as a phenomenon and with its causes ultimately makes truth inaccessible and the possibility of rationality an illusion. As a result, there will be no way of distinguishing the activities of scientists from their counterparts with rather different methods. Science may not be the *whole* arbiter of truth, but once its claim to truth in its particular sphere is rejected, we are well on the way to nihilism. Barnes' reference to 'knowledge sources' makes it look as if he is succumbing to the temptation of the sociologist to treat what passes for knowledge solely as a cultural phenomenon. This leaves no room for asking whether it really is knowledge. We ought, too, to be wary about accepting the analogy with false belief. Causal explanations may sometimes be forthcoming to explain why someone fell into error. Even someone rejecting rigid determinism may accept this, and also that we may be able to produce causal factors as to why someone arrived at the truth at one time rather than another. The fact of belief, though, and not its falsity (or truth) is being explained. Causal explanations of error show why someone fell into error, and not that it is error. Explanations of false belief presuppose that we are already confident that we can distinguish falsity and truth. If this is totally the product of social conditioning, rather than the result of our exercise of rationality and of the accessibility of reality, the sunlit meadows of relativism beckon. Unfortunately they soon slope down to the abyss of nihilism.

The sociologist's approach to science is sometimes illuminating. Investigations of the interactions of scientists, their career-structure, the effect of government financing, the function of learned journals and so on may well tell us something of how science develops. Yet we are left with the conviction that there must be more to it than that. Science is not just what a group of men happens to do. The effect, and indeed the purpose, of Barnes' analysis is to remove the notions of truth as the goal, of reality as the subject matter, and of knowledge as the prize in science. This jettisoning of any idea of the rationality of scientific method in favour of a causal analysis of scientists' activity never faces the question as to what scientific enquiry is about. It may explain why the focus of scientific interest veers from one area to another but it never adequately explains the basic purpose of scientific investigation. What is being investigated? Without the possibility of research into the nature of reality, the practice of science seems pointless. Sociologists of science all too often seem to be carrying through a reductionist programme, whereby the practice of science is decided wholly in sociological terms. The snag is that if they are right about the character of science as merely a social institution, the scientists who accept what they say may well find their own activities very pointless. It is not wholly fanciful to suggest that the sociology of science could so undermine the practice of science that ultimately there would be no scientists left for sociologists to investigate.

Attacks by sociologists on the authority of science and scientific method have all too often been implicitly replacing natural science with sociology as the source of knowledge, even though the practice of sociology is just as vulnerable to causal explanation. Many sociologists do see that their arguments apply to themselves. Nevertheless the difficulty they refer to remains one even if we can say to them 'it applies to you too'. Why should causal explanation be restricted to the genesis of false beliefs? The advent of true beliefs also seems to require explanation. One answer is that it is too easy just to assume that false beliefs are completely susceptible of causal explanation. It is evidence of a rather touching faith in man's rationality, since it appears to be thought that man is always going to arrive at truth unless deflected by outside influences of which he will usually be unaware. The possibility of genuine irrationality is then ruled out, since no-one seems able to adopt a belief irrationally against the evidence, if all error is causally explicable. This kind of position in fact applies a determinist view to false belief and it is hardly surprising that sociologists have thought it consistent to adopt the same view about apparently true belief.

Questions of validity and justification are either important in cases of false *and* true belief or we have to give up any attempt to reason. External factors can at times explain the occurrences of *both* types of belief, and *any* judgement that they are true or false presupposes the possibility of rationality and of access to reality. The basic question is just whether the question of the justification for what is believed can be separated from the kind of causal explanation sometimes forthcoming for the *fact* of belief. Are questions of truth independent of those about causal antecedents? How fallacious is the genetic fallacy?

Philosophers of science have often wished to distinguish between the context of justification and that of discovery when there may be no recognized method. There are many ways of stumbling on the truth, while justification is thought to involve a deliberate rational assessment of the validity of a theory. Feyerabend is among those who would deny the distinction. He uses arguments from history and maintains[15] that the 'application of methods of criticism and proof which are said to belong to the context of justification would wipe out science as we know it, and would never have permitted it to arise'. The point is circular. If we grant that science has not always developed very rationally, but that it has been influenced by what Feyerabend refers to as 'psychological, socio-economic-political, and other "external" conditions' it follows that science 'as we know it today' is the result of these conditions. Whether contemporary science is science as it should be is another matter. We cannot be so parochial as to imagine that present-day science has defined the limit of what should count as knowledge, and much of what is now accepted will probably one day be seen as inadequate or even mistaken. It is double-edged to suggest, as Feyerabend does, that present-day science could not exist 'without a frequent overruling of the context of justification', since it may have been much improved if it had proceeded on a more rational basis. Feyerabend might answer this by saying that even those parts of science where we feel certain we possess knowledge developed in ways which would be ruled out by strict methodology. It has sometimes proved right, he would claim, to hold to a theory in the face of apparently weighty counter-evidence, even though at the time, given the evidence available, it was an irrational thing to do. 'Ideas', he claims, 'which today form the very basis of science exist only because there are such things as prejudice, conceit, passion: because these things opposed reason: and because they were permitted to have their way'.

It may sometimes pay to back a hunch and be swayed by the flimsier evidence. Traditional scientific method has doubtless been too ready to sacrifice a theory in the face of an apparent falsifying instance, whereas the theory may in fact be largely true. A simple explanation might one day be forthcoming for its apparent falsification in particular circumstances. Yet refusing to be concerned by the sum of the available evidence is a gamble. It may pay off, but more than pig-headedness is needed to justify it. One should rely, at the very least on *some* evidence for the truth of one's theory. Incorrigible prejudice is no doubt sometimes lucky, but could hardly be preferable to being guided by the evidence available. Men are not infallible, however careful they are in the pursuit of truth, and, on the other hand, sometimes stumble on the truth by chance. Feyerabend's conclusion is that we therefore need no scientific method. Yet we are surely more likely to make a true judgement if we attempt to do so than if we just hope something will turn up. A faulty method can be improved, and we must not forget that the aim of scientific method is to arrive at theories which show the world as it really is.

If the 'genetic fallacy' is not a fallacy, hope must be given up of aiming at a distinctive scientific method which can distinguish between what is relevant to truth and what is 'external'. We are then merely confronted with beliefs and their origins, and must concentrate on the concrete fact of men with beliefs, putting aside any concern for truth. The latter demands recognition of the genetic fallacy, which could indeed be said to justify the distinction between the history and the philosophy of science. The suggestion that there is no fallacy inevitably involves abandoning realism. It remains vital to distinguish between the fact of a belief being held and what the belief purports to be about. Trying to assess the content of a belief by invoking the social conditions which could have led to the holding of it is fallacious.

Significant Causal Chains

It is tempting to think that explaining beliefs in terms of causes is totally irrelevant to any question of their truth. One could then adopt the complete programme of the sociology of knowledge, and give sociological explanations of all beliefs, while thinking the questions of truth and validity remain untouched. For instance, a sociologist, J. D. Y. Peel[16] says:

> It is not legitimate for the scientist or rationalist to exempt his views from sociological analysis by saying 'I hold these views simply because the evidence demands it.' We want to know why he, of all people, has come to interpret the evidence in this way. Conversely, to give a causal account of a belief is not to undermine its validity: it just is not relevant to it.

Is this right? The sociology of knowledge has a striking tendency to undermine a realist understanding of truth and reality, and to turn instead to forms of idealism and even relativism. This was the case with Mannheim and Lukacs, and the same holds true for contemporary exponents of the discipline. An eagerness to give causal explanations of belief in sociological terms inevitably involves a willingness to treat all beliefs on an equal footing. Indeed one writer[17] defines what he terms the 'strong programme' of the sociology of knowledge by saying that it would be symmetrical in its style of explanation so that 'the same types of causes would explain true and false beliefs'. This results in a tendency to restrict the validity of the beliefs to those who hold them. For example, Barnes admits[18] that his work is 'relativistic because it suggests that belief systems cannot be objectively ranked in terms of their proximity to reality or their rationality'. He talks of the growth of knowledge and claims that 'the process can be understood deterministically, and that claims to validity throughout remain contingent, since any "context of justification" must always rest upon negotiated conventions and shared exemplars'. He is frank enough to admit that his own account of knowledge can have no special status and that what he says about validity applies to his own views. He started off his book by admitting that he was going to talk of knowledge as 'accepted belief', not 'correct belief', and it is apparent that his position makes it impossible to talk of truth apart from what people happen to accept as true. He is consistent enough to apply his determinism to himself and writes: 'A deterministic account of the creation of the arguments presented here is perfectly possible and acceptable. Even if that account cited "external" social factors, this need not influence the evaluation of the knowledge thereby explained.'

What is the relationship of determinism with questions of validity and truth? Determinists have often faced the objection that if determinism is true their belief in determinism is itself caused. This point rests on a view that a caused belief is somehow disqualified from being well-grounded in the way in which it is considered that rational belief ought to be. Anyone who wishes to say that a caused belief logically cannot be a true belief must be wrong. Brainwashing techniques can just as easily be used to inculcate true beliefs as false beliefs. It would be obvious nonsense to say that causal mechanisms play no part in how we see the world, or otherwise come into contact with things outside themselves. We do not see the world in the way we do by accident, and perception is not simply a matter of judgement. We normally see what we do because of what is in front of us. We normally feel what we do because of what is in contact with our skin. Yet the fact that a perception is caused is no guarantee of its reliability. Drugs can induce hallucinations.

We need to be able to distinguish some causes from others. Some bring about true beliefs in us: others create false beliefs. How do we distinguish these types of cause? Even in the case of perception we need a criterion with which to distinguish truth from falsity, apart from an appeal to the fact of causation. It is even conceivable that my optic nerves be stimulated in such a way that I see (or think I see) rain at a time when it is actually raining. I would then correctly believe that it was raining, but the rain would not be the cause of my belief. We cannot equate a true belief that it is raining with a belief caused by the rain. It is a perennial problem that people can accidentally hit on the truth even though their route to it might be very idiosyncratic.

Some causal claims will be significant, and some will not be. We need an independent criterion of truth. It is not surprising that when we come to beliefs of a more complicated sort than mere perceptual beliefs, a causal account will raise similar questions. Determinists are fond of claiming that even if we accept the truth of determinism our understanding of rationality need not change. Indeed, they would say that causal explanation provides the model for all rational explanation. Yet, as with perception, not all causal chains leading to true belief are equally reliable. Plato gives an example in the *Theaetetus*[19] of the jury in a court of law who are led to certain beliefs by a skilful orator. They might in fact be led to believe what is true, but if the lawyer had been on the other side, he could just as easily have convinced them of the opposite.

Reason, Causes and Truth

Although causal mechanisms may be involved in our discovery of truth, it seems essential for us to be able to stand outside them and assess them. We need to know what is true before we can accept a certain causal chain as reliable. Even when we have distinguished the true beliefs from the false ones, and decided which true beliefs have their causal origin in the facts of the matter, and which have arrived at the truth purely fortuitously, we still have to decide which causal chain between the facts and the true belief is significant. There may even be causal links between the facts in a situation and a false belief. An eye-witness to an accident may be so upset by what he saw that he becomes confused and gives a totally mistaken account of what happened. The accident is almost directly linked with his false beliefs about it.

This last example serves to show that we must be very wary of accepting that the causal origins of a belief are in any way relevant to establishing its truth. I can believe what I do about a certain state of affairs *because* of that state of affairs and yet still be mistaken in my belief. It cannot be a sufficient condition for the truth of a belief that its origins lie in the facts of the particular matter. It is not a necessary condition either and this is shown very clearly by the existence of beliefs which are accidentally true. I could misread the time of a train, but fix on the correct time because I was referring to an out-of-date timetable.

Reasons can be causes. Rather than helping those who wish to give a deterministic explanation of belief and reasoning, this merely moves the basic problem back a stage. We still have to have a prior notion of the difference between 'genuine reasoning' and 'mere rationalization'. What is wrong with believing something because one wants it to be true? Why is that not a 'good reason'? If reasons and desires are equally described as possible causes, we are faced with a choice. We may treat them as identical kinds of thing, but then the distinction we may wish to draw between reasoning and rationalizing becomes impossible to make. On the other hand, we may insist on there being essential differences between them. In that case, the fact that each may have a causal role becomes irrelevant. We need a further criterion to distinguish between them, and we distinguish between them because of our concern for truth. Believing something because we want it to be true is not going to be a very reliable method of gaining knowledge. It is more sensible to have grounds for our belief, and these are our reasons. Rationalization is bad, precisely because it is likely to make us believe what we would like to be true, and not what probably is true.

The interesting question is not the relation between our reasons and our beliefs. The argument with the determinist typically comes when we ask why someone should count something as a reason, which another person thinks is no reason at all, or at least a very bad one. In such a case there is disagreement over evidence for what is true. The sociologist of knowledge will claim that there are sociological explanations forthcoming. He will say that the rejection of something as providing insufficient grounds for belief is the product of a causal chain, in just the same way as its acceptance as a basis for belief by someone else is also caused. What I count as good evidence, you may not, and this would be because of a different causal history. This means that the cause of our decisions about what to accept as evidence need have nothing to do with the question whether it is actually good evidence or not. Our reasons for belief will then have nothing to do with what is true, except fortuitously. They will still be connected with our judgements about what is true, but those judgements themselves may be caused by factors totally external to what is actually true.

If this account were correct, there would be no grounds for distinguishing between reasoning and mere rationalizing, since the basic purpose of the distinction has been removed. The possibility of rationality has been destroyed, if I can no longer be understood as weighing up evidence on its merits. Whatever my views of what is true may be, they are the product, it seems, of circumstances outside my control, and I am probably quite ignorant of them. It is thus completely accidental if my beliefs are true.

Each person will instead be causally predisposed to count certain things as evidence, and to favour certain outcomes to argument and discussion. The offering of reasons may convince an opponent in an argument, but not because they are good reasons and lead to truth. They might well be, but he will not be simply convinced by their validity. He will accept them because he has been socially conditioned to accept them as valid. The question whether they really are valid cannot be sensibly raised by determinists, apart from the question whether people think they are valid. If they do not, they may be induced to, but the distinction between rational persuasion and the techniques of persuasion can only be one between different ways of convincing people. There seems no good reason for preferring rational to non-rational methods, and the methods of, say, the slick advertiser may very well be more effective. The emotivists in ethics took this to heart and with their emphasis on the dynamic force of moral language left no room for dispassionate moral discussion.

Caused Belief

It might be tempting to say that determinism leads to the view that all reasoning is rationalization, and that reasons are completely bogus explanations. This would be unwarranted, since it is perfectly possible for a causal chain to proceed through the reasons we have for our beliefs and actions. The fact that we have this or that particular reason could be the cause of our belief. I would probably give up the belief if I changed my mind about the reason. Nevertheless all reasoning would come to share an important feature with rationalization. Its essential links with truth would be broken. Just as I may believe something because I want it to be true and not because I have reasons for thinking it is true, I may believe something because I am caused to believe I have grounds for thinking it true. In each case my belief is the product of something which is completely external to the question whether my belief may or may not be true. I may want to believe in the truth of what is in fact false, and I can be caused to think that a belief is well-grounded when in fact it is based on very flimsy evidence. The reverse is also the case. I may as a result of wishful thinking and without adequate reasoning come to believe what is in fact true, and in the same way, I can be caused to believe what is true.

How can we tell who is caused to believe what is true as opposed to what is false? How can we see who is in possession of knowledge and who has hit on the truth by accident? We must obviously have a prior understanding of what is true and of what constitutes good reasons for belief. This presupposes that we somehow stand outside the determinist system, since the whole problem has been merely shifted back a stage if *we* ourselves are to be understood as merely caused to believe some things and disbelieve others. If we believe a certain causal chain is significant and provides a basis for knowledge, this is because of our understanding of the situation, and in particular our belief as to what is true. These themselves, according to the determinist, must be caused.

The point is not that people are more likely to be wrong in what they believe, according to determinism, but that their beliefs, even if true, are not grounded in reality. They are merely caused to view reality in a certain way, and the sociology of knowledge claims that social factors are of primary importance here. Reality may be as they think it is, but when others are caused to view reality in a different way, rational discussion between the parties to the dispute would be beside the point. Countervailing causes are needed to influence one side. The problem then arises why the different groups need even to come to an agreement. When agreement is produced by the most effective causes rather than by a convergence of belief produced by a rational process, it is certainly no use as a guide to truth. The most effective methods of changing belief are not necessarily those that bring about true beliefs.

The essence of determinism is that we can never break out of the network of causes, in order to grasp reality as it is, rather than merely as we are caused to see it. Determinism makes the process of arriving at truth a haphazard one. In a non-determinist system the whole point of reasoning and assessing evidence is to decide what is true, and even though mistakes occur, it is not an accident that beliefs are true or that knowledge is gained. Determinism cannot adequately explain this, but must accept that the gaining of knowledge is a matter of chance. Even when I think the belief rests on sound evidence, I must acknowledge that my assessment of the evidence as good is itself causally produced. Needless to say, the fact that a belief is causally produced does not mean that it is not my belief or that I am holding it against my will. What it does mean is that I am holding it as a result of factors which may be totally unconnected with questions of truth or falsity. The determinist cannot recognize that what some one believes and why he believes it are totally different questions. Even if someone has a true belief, and bases it on good evidence, thinking it to be good evidence, the determinist must still hold that there is a causal explanation why this is so. Such an explanation may, for instance, refer to the society of which a man is a member and show he has been conditioned to think in that particular way. He may just as easily have been conditioned to think totally differently and weigh evidence differently (as people with a different upbringing might) and so the determinist's explanation merely shows why he thinks like that, and not why he thinks what is true. It is misrepresenting the determinist to say that the man holds his belief *because* he has good grounds. He rests his belief on grounds which he considers good as a result of some other causal background. The determinist is never in a position to pass from which reason a man may consider good, to which reasons *are* good. He may certainly *call* what he himself considers a good reason for belief simply 'a good reason' but he should remember that his views too must have been causally produced.

The same argument holds good for the determinist's belief in determinism. If determinism is true, that belief is as much causally explicable as any other belief. In principle, causal explanations can also be given for people's persistent adherence to doctrines about free-will. There is no rational way of deciding whose judgements are correct. That decision itself would be causally produced. Some people will be caused to agree, and others to disagree, but no-one can reach any conclusion which may not have been produced by external factors. Even if the evidence for its truth seems conclusive, it can always be argued that of course we are caused to judge the evidence conclusive, and this is unreliable, because others are doubtless caused to judge the same evidence inconclusive. The notion of 'evidence' must collapse into 'what people judge to be evidence', just as truth becomes 'what is judged to be true', and 'knowledge' becomes 'what is thought to be knowledge'. Determinists are in a quandary. Talk of 'demonstration', 'proof', 'evidence', and so on all involves reference to standards of rationality which presupposes a non-determinist background. It seems that rational arguments for determinism should not in all consistency be offered. If it is true, what brings men to believe it may have nothing to do with the merits of the case, and if it is false, apparently good arguments for it will be misleading. Determinism and the possibility of rationality are alternatives. Rationality presupposes the ability to see the truth for what it is without being influenced by extraneous considerations, and in a determinist system this is impossible.

Perhaps, it may be suggested, what is wrong is the notion of truth with which we have been operating. To make truth totally independent of man's beliefs is to face the possibility that all man's beliefs may be mistaken. Could we all be wrong? What sense could be given to the notion of a truth which is perhaps inaccessible? Maybe we should start from what people agree about, and make truth depend on human agreement. In other words, if we rely on a different theory of truth from a correspondence theory, the same problems may not arise. We need not worry then about the possible unreliability of our beliefs because of their causal origins. That would be irrelevant. We would merely have to try to achieve consistency between our own different beliefs and hope to achieve a large measure of agreement between men. If major disagreement between groups of people seems inescapable, then relativism would seem very attractive to a determinist. This is precisely the conclusion many sociologists of knowledge have reached.

We have said that determinism could be true. Paradoxically, this is itself to rely on the view of truth which we have indicated that determinism may have to give up. If most people are not determinists, but we say that determinism may provide a correct view of the world, we are still holding to the view that what people agree about and what is the case are two distinct notions. We are not merely saying when we hold that determinism may be true, that one day everyone will be determinists. We are claiming that there might in fact be very good reasons for them to adopt determinism. What everyone believes is not necessarily what there is reason to believe. We may on the other hand adopt any position which removes the possibility of talking about what might be true when a minority, or even nobody, believes it, or when it does not fit in very well with many of our other beliefs. It is then difficult to see what is being claimed when it is suggested that determinism could be true. To give this claim content, it seems essential to retain a view of truth which separates reality and men's conception of it.

Many determinists might agree that the attempt to explain all beliefs sociologically carries within it the seeds of its own destruction, and that without the ability to distinguish between significant and non-significant causal chains by appeal to some criterion any notion of objective truth is impossible. They might, however, claim that this is a point against sociologists of knowledge rather than determinists as such. What is the position of a determinist who, for example, thinks that evolution and natural selection have ensured that our beliefs do, by and large, match our environment, and that our beliefs are generally reliable, even though causally produced? In the same way, our ability to reason, use logic, and to distinguish between the reliability of different causal chains could have been causally produced. Such a determinist might feel that determinism is actually compatible with the exercise of our rationality.

Even this position rests on a belief in evolution, which its proponent is presumably predisposed causally to accept, if determinism is true. The determinist must accept that at some point he is caused to accept the one position and his opponents another, whatever the merits of the case may be. His opponents need not in that case feel under any obligation to accept what he says. Even if it *is* true, why should they feel that they ought to shake off their own predispositions to suit his? They would anyway not be free to do so at will. When there is disagreement, even if it does not occur until a fundamental level, determinism cannot allow that there is any need or indeed any possibility of resolving it rationally. Different groups of people can be made to agree by various means, but that is a different question from that of the rational resolution of a dispute. It is no accident that the sociology of knowledge in its typical form has seen that explanations of disagreement solely in terms of causes inevitably leads to a revision of our ideas of rationality and truth.

6 REALITY AND QUANTUM MECHANICS

The Attraction of Idealism

The last chapter showed the perils of assuming that our judgements about the world are totally determined. Yet the very developments in physics in this century which have suggested that rigid determinism cannot account for the behaviour of sub-atomic particles also pose questions about their objectivity. There may of course be a prejudice current amongst physicists that the possibility of objectivity entails determinism. Do developments in quantum mechanics mean that a realist approach cannot be maintained at the sub-atomic level? The relationship between science and philosophy is complex, but no-one can maintain that scientific discoveries leave philosophy untouched. Philosophers look to science as a source of examples when they are talking of what can be known. Something has gone radically wrong if scientists discover that their findings do not tally with current philosophical views. As human knowledge increases and our understanding of physical reality grows, it will not be surprising if our philosophical position alters. Similarly, there is always the danger that scientists try to operate with the philosophy of a previous generation, and attempt to make empirical discoveries fit into a pattern which has already been discredited. We do not have to think that epistemology is merely a creature of its time or that its precepts, if valid, are not absolutely valid. We must not go to the other extreme and believe that it is so 'pure' a discipline that all empirical findings are irrelevant. On the contrary, when science and philosophy part company, one must be in error.

Many physicists imagine that quantum mechanics has

made realism intolerable. J. A. Wheeler refers to 'the indispensable place of the participating observer—as evidenced in quantum mechanics—in defining any useful concept of reality'. As a result, he is led to an explicitly idealist position, and speculates 'how the observations of all the participators, past, present and future, join together to define what we call reality'. He continues:[1]

> Quantum mechanics has led us to take seriously and explore the . . . view that the observer is as essential to the creation of the universe as the universe is to the creation of the observer . . . Unless the blind dice of mutation and natural selection lead to life and consciousness and observership at some point down the road, the universe could not have come into being in the first place; . . . there would be nothing rather than something.

This is a puzzling view and Wheeler does not always make it clear that he is making a philosophical point about the definition of reality rather than a scientific one connecting the size and nature of the universe with the production of life and consciousness. Nevertheless he certainly concludes that reality cannot be logically independent of observation. How can an interpretation of quantum mechanics lead to this view?

The central problem is the perennial one of separating subject and object, observer and the reality observed. The non-separability of the micro-object and the instrument measuring it, and indeed the non-separability of both from the conscious observer, are themes which recur in the writings of theoretical physicists. We should not be very surprised at this emphasis on consciousness, because if science is thought to be about observations, as positivism has asserted, it requires the presence of observers. Observations do not exist on their own. They are what observers have. Even potential observations require potential observers. W. Heitler describes the situation as follows:[2]

It is clear that we can speak of a measurement as fully made and completed with all that it implies, only if we commonly take cognisance of the result . . . In the whole logical structure of quantum mechanics, the conscious observer plays an essential part. Man in so far as he is an observer can no longer be ignored.

He also writes:

The observer has become indispensable: a clear-cut separation of the external world from the observer is not possible as soon as any observations whatever are made: for these influence the object in an unpredictable way. Why the impossibility of separating object and subject should first appear just in the physics of the smallest particles is a question we cannot answer.

The trouble is that it is impossible to make measurements of a sub-atomic physical system without disturbing it in some way. The measuring instruments have a significant influence on the particles being measured. When it is also assumed that measurements have not genuinely been made until someone has become conscious of the results, it becomes tempting to envisage an amalgamation of system, instrument and observer rather than of an observer separated from the independent reality he is observing. Indeed, once we think of an observer being tied in with what is being observed, the very term 'observation' seems inappropriate. As a result, Wheeler is able to write:[3]

Participation is the incontrovertible new concept given by quantum mechanics: it strikes down the term 'observer' of classical theory, the man who stands safely behind the thick glass wall and watches what goes on without taking part. It can't be done, quantum mechanics says. Even with the lowly electron, one must participate before we can give any meaning whatsoever to its position or momentum.

There are two issues here which must always be kept

separate. The first is that instruments causally affect what is being measured at the sub-atomic level. Such influences are irrelevant at the level of classical physics, but are of crucial importance when the electron is being investigated. A realist will not be surprised at such an effect, but it is irrelevant to the truth of realism. Talk of the causal effect of the instrument on an electron presupposes that the one can in principle be separated from the other. Theoretical physicists, however, are not just talking of the interference the act of measurement makes at the sub-atomic level. They question the possibility of logically distinguishing between measurement and thing measured. The dualism of subject and object, of observer and reality, is again being questioned, this time because of the results obtained by working scientists.

It is notorious that quantum mechanics can only discover regularities of a statistical sort in sub-atomic systems. There seems to be an essential indeterminism in the behaviour of particles, which is irrelevant to any question of the possibility of an objective reality. Yet this is also put in question by the very nature of quantum mechanics. One physicist says:[4] 'Most of all, as has been particularly emphasized by Einstein, it is the notion of the objective reality of the physical world, the cornerstone of all classical physics, which has become practically obliterated in the new physics.'

We must investigate in greater detail how this could have come about. First, what precisely *is* quantum mechanics? It has been described as follows:[5]

> Quantum mechanics consists essentially of a set of mathematical rules which should give at least in principle, the solution of the following problem: specified certain conditions on the system of interest (elementary particle, atom, molecule etc.), or more schematically, given the result of a first observation made on it at a time $t = 0$, calculate the probability that a second observation gives a certain other result after a time t. Quantum mechanics does not describe a system

in itself, but only deals with the results of actual observations on it. Due to the central role of observation, an understanding of the process of measurement is of fundamental importance in quantum mechanics.

I am concerned with the philosophic presuppositions of quantum mechanics and not its formulation, although the latter may of course influence the former. The very fact that it deals with 'measurements' or 'observations' (and uses these terms synonymously) already builds in a bias against realism. Indeed, E. P. Wigner[6] inclines to the view that the equations of motion of both classical theory and quantum mechanics are not 'descriptions of reality, but only a means for calculating the probabilities of the outcomes of observations'. He comments that 'most of us' are positivists, that a positivist's main concern is observations, and these are the impressions he receives. It is hardly surprising that this view gives rise to the notion, also mentioned by Heitler, that a measurement is only completed where it enters the consciousness of an observer. This is an extension of the view that a system does not possess certain attributes prior to measurement, but that they appear as a result of and simultaneously with measurement. Now it seems that they only appear when someone takes note of the measurement. Wigner writes:[7]

> It is the entering of an impression into our consciousness which alters the wave function because it modifies our appraisal of the probabilities for different impressions which we expect to receive in the future. It is at this point that the consciousness enters the theory unavoidably and unalterably. If one speaks in terms of the wave function, its changes are coupled with the entering of impressions into our consciousness.

It is hardly surprising that Wigner concludes[8] that idealism provides the best 'concept of the real' and says that 'excepting immediate sensations and, more generally, the content of my consciousness, everything is a construct'.

A positive preoccupation with observations blends with an operationalist concentration on measurements. Operationalism is very much in tune with the down-to-earth prejudices of working physicists. It holds that symbols, whether words or figures, only have meaning in so far as they concern possible human operations. Science is therefore about what men can do rather than about the reality they are investigating. It might not be altogether clear as a result why they are doing what they are doing, but that is by the way. Physics is concerned with measurements themselves rather than with any reality being measured.

According to most physicists, observations and measurements are the preoccupation of quantum mechanics, but there are several possible interpretations of the precise relationship of the various parts of the amalgam of system, instrument and observer. Wigner's method is in effect to reduce the first two to the last, and it is interesting to note how many physicists in the past, including Mach and Eddington, have been tempted by idealism. Other interpretations have stressed the non-separability of system and instrument, perhaps bringing in the observer as well, without suggesting that the observer is in some sense logically prior. Nevertheless, from the realist point of view, the logical inseparability of 'subject' and 'object' to the point that they have to be regarded as a solid block, is as unwelcome as the idealist reduction of anything to what can be observed. The independent existence of physical objects (however small) is at risk in both cases.

There is a danger, in fact, in quantum mechanics that more attention is paid to scientists and their operations than to physical reality. According to Wheeler,[9] the quantum principle says 'No physics without an observer.' There is a sense in which this is trivially true, since our knowledge of the world is built up through observations, and physical science is the systematization of man's knowledge. Yet the phrase can also suggest that physical reality itself is in some way dependent on observation, and that it is self-contradictory to refer to endurable entities. This is the crux of the difficulty in quantum mechanics, and it is why it is in many respects a test case for realism. Empiricism is by definition opposed to reference to entities which have a wholly theoretical status, even though today's theoretical entities may with technological progress become tomorrow's observed ones. Nevertheless, there is a distinction between theoretical and experimental physics. Experiments, observations and measurements all involve a subject and an object. Someone is observing, and something is being observed. Someone is measuring, and something is being measured. When the act of measurement itself disturbs the object, there may be a case for wondering just how to draw the boundary between subject and object. Yet none of this is connected with the basic task of theoretical physics which is to describe the nature of physical reality. Reference to a subject, as observer or in any other capacity, is irrelevant. Excessive concern with observation can result in making theoretical physics a nonsubject. There would be no means of distinguishing it from experimental physics.

Continued references to the importance of consciousness have another important result. It looks as if sciences about men must underlie any understanding of 'the world', if the scope of science is made explicitly dependent on man's capabilities. Yet even these sciences will presumably depend on man's consciousness. As Wheeler himself remarks—'consciousness can analyse the world around, but when will consciousness understand consciousness?'. We seem to be involved in the most disheartening of vicious circles. It is interesting that Wheeler's way of putting the problem itself presupposes some kind of distinction between consciousness and 'the world around'. The problem is just how we can any longer give sense to the notion of a 'world around' for consciousness to analyse. Physicists dealing with quantum mechanics would be the last to accept that consciousness was operating in a complete vacuum, or that their theories were the result of total creativity on their part.

They are constrained by what actually happens. Indeed their departure from classical mechanics is not the result of a whim or a feeling that it might be nice to have a change. Since quantum mechanics transcends national and ideological boundaries, it seems implausible to explain its existence in sociological terms. Wheeler would hold that his emphasis on consciousness is necessary because of the way the world is. Since the existence of consciousness is itself an objective matter, reference to it could itself embody a correct theory of reality. An idealist position need not be a subjectivist one. At the same time, consciousness is *discovering*, and not producing, the behaviour of elementary particles. This point must be decisive against any slide to an exclusively anthropocentric position. Some physicists, like Wigner and Wheeler, may find it very tempting to reach a view which so denies the reality of anything apart from consciousness that the universe itself appears to draw its reality from our own existence. The very constraints which have led them to this suggest that there is a reality beyond our consciousness, and its strange behaviour has led us from classical to quantum mechanics. As a result, some form of dualist position, at the very least, seems necessary in order that subject and object be adequately distinguished.

Objectivity and Instruments

Quantum mechanics is faced with constraints which never troubled classical mechanics. It is very tempting to give a description of an objective state of affairs, the state of an atom, in the same way that classical mechanics described a world which it regarded as having an independent and determinate existence. Words such as 'measurement', 'position', 'energy', 'temperature', all derive from classical physics and carry its assumption of objectivity. We must be very careful not to beg the question and use such words with their classical implications unless we are very sure of our right to do so. An insistence on the importance of objectivity in quantum mechanics does not entail that its objective world is similar in composition and behaviour to the world at macro-level which classical machanics deals with. Since both are concerned with different levels of the same world, we must not allow them to be incompatible, but dissimilar systems are not necessarily incompatible ones.

This question of the relationship between classical and quantum mechanics is a crucial one. Many physicists would find no difficulty in ascribing objectivity to the measuring devices used and to the results they give. As a result, one possible way out would be to ascribe reality to those, rather than to the micro-level they purport to be measuring. Another possibility is to treat the microsystem and instruments as an indivisible whole. One physicist suggest the following can be held:[10] 'That a microsystem makes up an indivisible whole together with the instruments that produce and analyse it, that it thus does not have—except by convention—properties that are its own and that consequently it is not a "full-fledged" system.'

He calls this the principle of object-instrument non-separability. He points out[11] that the principles of conventional quantum theory contain explicit reference to measuring instruments. As a result, it looks as if these principles are concerned with intersubjective validity rather than with the objectivity of what is being measured. He says that if we wish to continue to talk of reality which is the *source* of man's experience, then we are to admit that 'such a reality does *not* obey the principle of separability' and 'the atomistic description of events and/or micro-objects is obviously just a model'. Thus an apparatus may be used, but its atomic constituents cannot have an automonous existence.

A major figure in the development of quantum mechanics has been Niels Bohr. He faced the question whether it was possible to retain the epistemology of classical physics and concluded that the language of physics must remain classical, with certain limitations. He emphasized the following:[12]

> However far the phenomena transcend the scope of classical physical explanation, the account of all evi-

dence must be expressed in classical terms . . . This crucial point . . . implies the impossibility of any sharp separation between the behaviour of atomic objects and the interaction with the measuring instruments which serve to define the conditions under which the phenomena appear . . . Consequently, evidence obtained under different experimental conditions cannot be comprehended within a single picture, but must be regarded as complementary in the sense that only the totality of the phenomena exhausts the possible information about the objects.

Bohr's notion of complementarity involves the use of contrasting pictures which are incompatible with each other but which each refer to what he calls 'an essential aspect of empirical evidence'. He gives as an example the dilemma concerning the corpuscular and wave properties of electrons and photons. It is impossible to ascribe both position and momentum to atomic objects simultaneously, since the measurement of one precludes the measurement of the other because of interaction with the apparatus. In giving an account of one experimental arrangement Bohr comments[13] that 'we are presented with a choice of either tracing the path of a particle or observing interference effects'.

He wishes to regard the combination of apparatus and atomic object as an indissoluble unity. The object cannot be referred to as separate from the instruments measuring it. He has a holistic view of the two, and is directly challenging the dichotomy between subject and object, at least when it might split apart the macro- and micro-levels. He wishes to insist that quantum phenomena can only be talked about as occurring in conditions specified by means of classical concepts. There is no reason why this position should lead to idealism unless the place of the observer is stressed. The measuring instruments are accessible to everyone. It is just that they cannot clearly be differentiated from what they are measuring, and as a result any notion of the self-subsistent reality of atomic objects has to be jettisoned. This is the conclusion many physicists draw, although talk of 'interaction' and of 'interference' certainly suggests a causal relationship between different entities. It could be replied that this is an illustration of the difficulty of talking about quantum mechanics in classical language. Nevertheless, Bohr's idea of an indivisible whole seems somewhat mystical. Granted that it is impossible to discover both the position and the momentum of a particle, and that investigation of the one precludes knowledge of the other, can we say that 'it' has both if we cannot discover both? Bohr's notion even stops us asking *what* is being measured. We have to be content with the fact of measurement. Consequently there appears to be no more sense in asking for something which lies beyond measurement. If we choose to investigate the momentum of a particle, we cannot even think that it *has* a position. The verificationist undertones in this are clear enough. Quantum mechanics seems more concerned with correlating observations or measurements than with theorizing about the nature of fundamental physical reality. Indeed the former is its avowed purpose.

According to Bohr, microscopic systems have no intrinsic properties. The reality observed is combined with the method of observation, and language can proceed on the level of classical physics. A realist position which holds that quantum reality has its own nature independent of observation or interference makes this approach very unsatisfying. Bohr is in effect ducking the basic problem. This is fundamentally a philosophical dispute, and physicists will, consciously or unconsciously, have to come down on one side or another. The refusal to face it and the decision to deal with measurements and the prediction of measurements, on a probabilistic basis, is a *de facto* decision to adopt the anti-realist position. One answer may be that working physicists are not philosophers, and while philosophy may be concerned with metaphysical speculation, physicists are restricted to what is actually and possibly within their reach.

Quantities that cannot in principle be measured are of no interest to them. Even a realist physicist would have to ignore them. There is some truth in this, but many physicists do find philosophical speculation about what they are doing and researching into essential to their task. Philosophy may not directly affect what a physicist does, but it is certainly relevant to his understanding of what he is doing and his purpose in doing it.

One physicist[14] asks if there is any sense in asking what an electron is actually doing when we cannot observe it. He comments that 'most physicists and philosophers would agree in saying that you must not ask questions if you know it is impossible to find the answer'. We are certainly doomed to a totally anthropocentric view, if we accepted this. We are confined to what we have access to. Indeed, in the case of quantum physics, we may even be confined to what it is at present empirically possible for us to find out. We may very well be precluded in such circumstances from asking about something which future generations may find accessible. According to the physicist just quoted, the attitude amongst working physicists is usually as follows:

> Since physics is concerned with understanding the observable world, it is enough to devise a system of thought (in other words a theory) which correlates different observations, and which allows future observations to be predicted from present knowledge. It is sufficient that the technique of prediction should work; it need not imply any explanation of the connection between cause and effect.

This is very obviously what is happening in quantum mechanics. Many of its practitioners believe it is not concerned with reality as such, but only with what a physicist may find when he makes a measurement. Henry Margeneau insists that quantum mechanics never refers to quantities of systems. He says:[15] 'All it does is to say, in probability terms, what may be found when a measurement is made.' It is, in other words, concerned with our knowledge and possible knowledge of reality, rather than with the nature of reality itself. Reality becomes inaccessible and measurements and observations stand in its place. The snag with this position is that it leaves the status of that reality unresolved.

Einstein's View of the Incompleteness of Quantum Mechanics

Quantum mechanics raises very clearly the whole question of the relationship between experience, theory and reality. Apologists for a realist position have not been lacking, although the so-called Copenhagen interpretation, exemplified by Bohr, has undoubtedly found most favour. Einstein himself was very unhappy about Bohr's position, and in a famous paper, raised the basic issues about the status of quantum mechanical description.[16] He started off with a statement of the realist distinction between reality and our understanding of it:

> Any serious consideration of a physical theory must take into account the distinction between the objective reality, which is independent of any theory, and the physical concepts with which the theory operates. These concepts are intended to correspond with the objective reality, and by means of these concepts we picture this reality to ourselves.'

Einstein emphasizes that any theory has to be both correct and complete. He says:'The correctness of the theory is judged by the degree of agreement between the conclusions of the theory and human experience. This experience, which alone enables us to make inferences about reality, in physics takes the form of experiment and measurement.'

While experience or experiment is vital in testing the truth of the theory, a realist will allow that theory can outstrip experience. Although Einstein's remarks are unexceptionable in the sense that experience does provide us with our only criteria for *judging* the correctness of a theory, we must be very careful not to lapse into saying that the correctness of theory *consists* in the degree of agreement between theory and experience. Whatever the precise relationship of our ideas with reality, what makes them correct is *reality*, the way things are, and not our experience of the way things are. This simple distinction is the crucial one which divides realism from more anthropocentric views. The realist is concerned with truth and not merely our judgements of truth. Many will no doubt be exasperated by this and ask what use 'truth' is if we do not at the time have access to it. We are concerned with *our* judgements and the criteria for them, and not, it may be held, with what might be the case even though we do not know it. Yet this leaves out of account the fact that we are aiming at truth in our judgements. We have changed the name of the game if the criteria we adopt in making them are totally unrelated to questions of objective truth or falsity.

This is exactly the issue in quantum mechanics. Einstein wished to argue that quantum mechanical description is incomplete. He asserted that in the case of a successful theory 'every element of the physical reality must have a counterpart in the physical theory'. Margeneau offers this criticism of the requirement:[17] 'One finds nowhere a concise exposition of the meaning of physical reality apart from physical theory: indeed it is my conviction that reality cannot be defined except by reference to successful physical theory. If this is true, Einstein's proposition becomes tautological, as I suspect it to be.'

This objection is yet again a version of the view that we only have access to reality through our concepts and theories, with no independent route to it. It is in fact a tautology to say, as Margeneau does, that only 'successful physical theory' can define reality, but this cloaks an important dispute. Is physical theory successful because it reflects reality correctly, or is reality what successful theory delineates? There is a substantial difference between these two positions, since the latter could very well be relying on a notion of 'success' which does not involve the notion of an independent reality. It could merely contain an appeal to experiment and measurement. In that case a successful theory would merely be one which agrees with our experience. That would not be understood just as a test of success, it would be what we *meant* by success. According to this view, reality is built up by theories which rest on *our* experience. It is hardly surprising if the unmeasurable and unobservable is thus ruled out as having no place in 'reality'. On the other hand, if we take the former position, as Einstein obviously wishes, it will not be obvious that experience, as shown in experiment and measurement, exhausts reality. This is all of crucial importance in quantum mechanics since the building up of reality from experience rules out the possibility of any part of reality being inaccessible. What cannot be measured does not exist. Einstein notes that the concept of state is the fundamental concept in quantum mechanics and it is supposed 'to be completely characterized by the wave function ψ, which is a function of the variables chosen to describe the particle's behaviour'. Certain unknowable quantities cannot be real if quantum mechanics gives a complete description of reality. For example, a particle cannot be assumed to have momentum in certain circumstances. As Einstein points out, the fact that a measurement disturbs a particle and alters its state means that certain quantities are unobtainable. A complete theory ought to include them, since by definition it must reflect reality. Therefore, either quantum mechanics is incomplete, or 'when the operators corresponding to two physical quantities do not commute, the two quantities cannot have simultaneous reality'. What is not in the theory is not real. He remarks:

> In quantum mechanics, it is usually assumed that the wave function *does* contain a complete description of the physical reality of the system in the state to which it corresponds. At first sight, this assumption is entirely reasonable, for the information available from a wave

function seems to correspond exactly to what can be measured without altering the state of the system.

Einstein is not happy with this postition, and not only wants to aim for the objectivity of the quantities concerned, but wishes to link that with predictability. He proposed the following as a criterion of reality: 'If, without in any way disturbing a system, we can predict with certainty (i.e. with probability equal to unity) the value of a physical quantity, then there exists an element of physical reality corresponding to this physical quantity.'

He and his colleagues wisely suggest that this is a sufficient and not a necessary condition of reality, since it would be a very large assumption to suppose that *all* parts of reality are predictable. Indeed even the view that if something is predictable that proves its reality, depends on metaphysical views about the regularity of what happens in nature. If, after all, the latter actually behaved in a chaotic and random way, our good fortune in obtaining what were apparently successful predictions would be profoundly misleading. Predictability depends on regularity. Saying this demonstrates that discussions about predictability *presuppose* the independent reality of what is predictable. It may be true that if something be predictable, it is real, but this is because we have already assumed that predictability must have a basis in a feature of reality. Success in prediction may give us confidence that we have stumbled on reality. Saying that it is a 'sufficient condition of reality' may be somewhat misleading, since, strictly speaking, it is irrelevant to the question of what reality is, even if it may follow from one of the characteristics it often possesses. Perhaps this is unfair since Einstein is only pointing to one way of *recognizing* reality. Nevertheless, the criterion is a somewhat unfortunate one in the context of quantum mechanics, since it suggests that predictability and determinate behaviour are linked with questions of reality and objectivity. Yet an inability to predict the behaviour of particles or to determine their position or momentum does not prove that they are not real. It does not entail that it is meaningless to assume that they have any position or momentum. There could be a genuine inde-terminacy in nature at the sub-atomic level. Our inability to predict may not just be the result of enforced ignorance. It may stem from the way things are. It is significant that when indeterminacy is talked about in quantum mechanics, it is often not made clear whether the indeterminacy lies in our knowledge of the way things are or in the things themselves. Is our knowledge doomed to be imprecise or is there no basis in nature for any precision? The point is that this question itself arises from a realist position. Any distinction between restrictions placed on our knowledge and pecu-liarities in the behaviour of the entities of which we have knowledge presupposes that reality is independent of know-ledge. No physicist influenced by positivism would accept that.

The Limitations of Classical Physics

Realism leaves open the possibility that the entities described in quantum mechanics possess unmeasurable quantities. They would not be logically inaccessible in some metaphysical realm. It is just that we cannot, for instance, simultaneously discover position and momentum. We can know either, but not both. Physicists have been too ready to assume the equivalence of reality with our knowledge of it. Nevertheless, realism is a philosophical position. It allows questions to be asked which would not otherwise be raised, and makes distinctions which would otherwise be ignored. It does not adjudicate between scientific theories. At the most, it might illuminate the interpretation of a theory. Einstein's question whether quantum mechanics offers a complete description of physical reality will obviously require re-ference to the relevant mathematics. A realist can, however, point to a possible equivocation in the word 'complete'. Einstein wanted a total reflection of physical reality in the theory. Once, though, someone holds that reality must be accessible and that unmeasurable quantities cannot be real, his view of reality becomes more restricted and his understanding of what would be included in a complete description is affected. If the description offered is the best that can in principle be obtained, then it is complete, since *ex hypothesi* there is nothing it has failed to include. When the notion that certain quantities are unobtainable but are nevertheless real is accepted, we can envisage the best description we can get still being incomplete. One's notion of completeness can itself depend on philosophical views about the nature of reality. There is the added complication of terminology that it might be perfectly possible to regard the best obtainable description as a 'complete' one, while recognizing that even a complete description does not exhaust the nature of reality.

Einstein's views hold open the possibility that an underlying mechanism might be found which would allow us to retain the rigid determinism of classical physics. Most physicists would now reject this. Heitler, for instance, says,[18] 'I believe it has been proved that quantum mechanics, when put on an axiomatic basis, is *logically complete* and permits therefore no such underlying mechanism.' J. S. Bell[19] says: 'No local deterministic hidden-variable theory can reproduce all the experimental predictions of quantum mechanics.' The search for 'hidden variables' is getting more and more to seem a forlorn one. Without them, quantum theory includes a basic indeterminism, although this is balanced by a kind of statistical determinism which ensures that classical determinism is still valid for physical reality at the macroscopic level.

The assumption that there are no hidden variables may entail indeterminism, but what is its effect on the notion of strong objectivity? Once it is recognized that objectivity and determinism are two separate issues, the question of the relationship between observer, apparatus and reality is still a live one. We have to come to terms with the essential discontinuities which must be seen as part of the elementary processes. Exhaustive causal descriptions are clearly to be ruled out, as are precise spatio-temporal ones. This does not put the question of independent reality at risk except for those whose notion of reality is linked indissolubly with classical deterministic views. Indeed it *follows* from what we take to be the nature of reality at the microscopic level. The puzzling ambivalence between wave and particle can be seen to have its origins in a feature of the world at the level of elementary particles. It is sheer positivist prejudice to deny both position and momentum to a particle merely because of our inability to measure both. Nevertheless, we should not be too ready to think that elementary particles are just like individual things at the macroscopic level, only smaller, and that they *must* have definite quantities. We can preserve the belief of classical physics in an independent reality without assuming that it must behave in just the way classical physics would expect. Any conclusions we draw must be derived from the way we take reality to behave and not merely from the possibility of making certain observations. One physicist says:[20]

> The assumption of a real outside world and the possibility of describing it are not contradicted by the laws of quantum physics. The question is only how the outside world may be carved up into pieces to which one may still attribute an objective individuality and real attributes.

Referring to particles with definite position and momentum involves us in the assumption that the microscopic world is a miniature copy of the macroscopic one. It is very easy to assume that the notion of objective reality, in science, at least, is defined by classical physics. The consequence of this is the overthrow of the whole concept of objectivity in a particular area, if classical physics is shown not to apply to it. Once we recognize that classical concepts may not provide adequate descriptions for the whole of material reality and we prise the notion of material reality apart from the world as described in classical physics, we are free to recognize that reality may take forms which our present conceptual scheme cannot describe. Arguments about whether something is a particle or a wave will inevitably be beside the point, since both are concepts from classical physics. Disputes about which classical concept is most appropriate become somewhat fatuous if reality is non-classical at the microscopic level.

In a sense, Bohr recognized this problem, but instead of stressing the limitations of classical concepts in the face of a non-classical reality, he restricted what can be meaningfully said to the limits set by our classical concepts. Reality, he thought, is describable and knowable only by means of the concepts we use in experiments conducted within the framework of classical physics. This means that the world of the atom must be conceived as *we* are able to comprehend it, and not as a thing-in-itself to which we may have no access. As always, when distinctions are made between reality-in-itself and reality-for-us, the reality of the former is put at risk. There is little doubt that Bohr was tempted to concentrate on what is accessible and even on just our conceptions of it to such an extent that in the end he was prepared to deny the reality of anything beyond. He was prepared to talk of our knowledge, without stopping to consider what we have knowledge *of*. He is quoted as saying the following:[21] 'There is no quantum world. There is only an abstract quantum mechanical description. It is wrong to think that the task of physics is to find out how nature *is*. Physics concerns what we can say about nature.'

This repudiation of any ontology undermines the whole purpose of physics. What is the point of saying anything about nature, if we are not attempting to say how nature is? What, indeed, are we talking about anyway? Bohr was convinced that we cannot be governed in what we say by what we discover about reality. He accepts the limited nature of our conceptual framework and assumes that we must be imprisoned in it for ever. We cannot know what cannot be expressed in the concepts of classical physics. The opposite approach would accept the inadequacy of classical concepts in portraying sub-atomic reality, but would hold that this was a good example of how reality cannot always be made to conform with the presuppositions of our conceptual scheme. Whereas Bohr dismisses reality, it is equally possible to modify our concepts. There is no reason to suppose that a conceptual scheme should remain rigid and unyielding even in the face of puzzling phenomena which cannot be readily comprehended by means of our accustomed concepts.

Bohr's preference for epistemology rather than ontology is shared by many physicists. For instance, C. F. von Weizacker says the following:[22]

> Knowledge exists as well as matter exists, and knowledge is perhaps even more important because we know about matter in the form of knowledge, but we do not know about knowledge in the form of matter. It is not symmetrical. Knowledge is really the more basic concept. And knowledge means that things are the way we know them.

This is a curious argument, and its basic anthropocentricity is clear enough. We have no access to matter except through the knowledge we acquire. This is a tautology. Yet we could have no knowledge unless the matter existed. Once the separate existence of matter is admitted, it seems perverse to want to make it secondary to our knowledge in some unclear sense. It is tautological to say that things are the way we know them, since knowledge entails the reality of what is known. Such a claim, though, can easily open the door to idealism. We only have to ask how things are even when we have no knowledge of them. Can they exist only as we know them or can they have unknown characteristics? Once reality and our knowledge are pressed together too clearly, we soon get to the position where it is held that an entity's reality is the product of our knowledge.

It is not surprising that quantum mechanics raises these

issues, since its mathematical formalism gives rise to definite paradoxes when it is interpreted as applying to a reality which is unaffected by our knowledge of it. This goes beyond the mere difficulty of the process of measurement interfering with the very phenomena it is supposed to be measuring. Von Weizacker[23] himself points out that physicists want the 'state vector' (which contains all the information about the future that can be deduced from all observations so far made on the object) to be two things at once. They want to say that it portrays the objective state of things, and that it is an expression of our knowledge. He says: 'We will not expect contradictions if we stick to this rule: quantum theory is a theory on the probabilistic connection of facts. Facts themselves are to be described causally. Where a classical description is not possible there is no fact.'

We have here the association of causality with objectivity and the demand by definition that reality should conform to classical physics. No room is left for the possibility that material reality may behave very differently at the microscopic level from what classical physics would lead us to expect.

The Strangeness of Reality

It may be illuminating to examine one of the famous paradoxes produced by quantum physics, namely that of Schrödinger's cat. Schrödinger imagined, in the early days of quantum mechanics, an experiment where a cat and a flask of poison are enclosed together in a container. The breaking of the flask and the killing of the cat can be triggered by the discharge of a Geiger counter placed in one of the beams of a two-hole experimental set-up where there is a fifty per cent chance of its being activated by the discharge of one electron. D'Espagnat describes the situation as follows if an experiment is conducted when only one electron is emitted.[24]

Schrödinger then pointed out that under these conditions if the cat is considered as a quantum system and described by a wave function, its final state is necessarily a quantum superposition of the two states 'cat alive' and 'cat dead', so that it should in no case be considered as being alive *or* as being dead. This state of affairs goes on until an outside observer opens the container and looks inside, for it is only through the latter process that the wave pocket is reduced, and that in one case out of two, the cat is truly killed. Owners of cats will, however, generally agree with Schrödinger that this description is paradoxical.

In fact, physicists would generally take the cat's being or not being poisoned as itself a measurement, but this just exhibits their prejudice that states of macro-observables have a reality which possible states of micro-observables may not possess. The paradox illustrates the way in which the formulation of quantum mechanics allows for the wave function to represent two possibilities. Half the wave corresponding to the electron can be understood as passing through one slit, the other half as going through the other. The system is represented by a linear combination of two waves, one representing the cat being killed, the other as still alive. As Putnam says:[25]

> If the system is not interfered with prior to 1.00 p.m. then we will predict that at 1.00 p.m. the system will be in a state that is a superposition of 'live cat' and 'dead cat'. We then have to say that the cat is neither alive nor dead at 1.00 p.m. unless someone comes and looks, and that it is the act of looking that throws the cat into a definite state.

Such a result is clearly counter-intuitive but as Putnam comments, it involves a situation which arises whenever micro-cosmic uncertainty is amplified so as to affect something detectable by us. Any situation where a Geiger counter is employed by a wave produces analogous results. 'Since', Putnam says, 'the Geiger counter will click if a particle hits it and will not click if a particle does not hit it, then its state at the relevant instant well be represented by a wave that is the superposition of the waves corresponding to "click" and "no-click".'

An immediate common-sense reaction to this is that the waves represent our knowledge of the different possibilities, so that the system is really in one of the substates, but we do not happen to know which. Either the cat is alive or it is dead, whether we know or not. Can we transfer this assumption from the level of the macroscopic world to the microscopic one? Must it be the case that when two states are 'superposed', the system is really one of them? Waves can be superposed even when they are mutually incoherent. The cat cannot be both dead and alive. Are we to say, then, of its analogues at the microscopic level that they may not be in either mutually exclusive state? We must return to Einstein's concern that quantum mechanics may not be complete. Without hidden variables the wave representation must be understood as giving a *complete* description of reality. There is no room left for an appeal to ignorance. Even when we are left with conflicting possibilities, things are as quantum mechanical formulation says they are. It is easy to see the attraction of refusing to say anything about the cat before someone looks. Micro-entities cannot possess definite numerical values before measurement, if quantum mechanics is complete. This is not because of any positivist view, but it stems from the puzzling nature of reality itself, if we are to believe quantum mechanics. We are in fact left with a view which suggests that the observer by looking actually throws a system into a definite state. The mixture of 'live cat' and 'dead cat' is thrown by observation into, say, 'dead cat'. We are not saying that the cat is alive or dead, but we do not know which, nor that the cat's existence and its state is somehow logically dependent on our observation. What is being suggested is that the very act of observation or measurement itself has a causal impact on what is being measured, so that it throws it into a definite state. We must be careful, since though this may itself be consonant with realism, it can clearly lead to paradoxical conclusions. Putnam expresses the dilemma as follows :[26]

> If we cannot say anything about the values of micro-observables, when we are not making measurements, except *merely* that they exist . . . in the Schrödinger's cat case we will be able to say only that the swarm of particles making up the cat and the apparatus exists and that it will certainly take the form 'live cat' or the form 'dead cat' if a measurement is made, i.e. if somebody looks. We will not be able to say that the cat is either alive or dead, or for that matter that the cat is even a cat, as long as no-one is looking.

'Micro-observables' must have definite characteristics, since otherwise the character of microscopic objects seems inexplicable. A liquid could not *be* a liquid unless the micro-entities which compose it not merely existed, but behaved in particular ways. Once we start saying that the observer 'throws' something into a particular state, whereas it was not previously in any definite measurable state, we are obviously treading the path to idealism. The affinity of quantum mechanics to positions like that of Berkeley is clear, if the application of its formalism, without further assumptions about the reality of macro-observables, means that a cat is not a cat unless someone is looking at it. The two positions are not identical. Philosophical idealism makes claims about the mind-dependence of all physical reality. The paradoxes which arise from quantum mechanics may encourage this view, but they spring from oddities which seem deeply rooted in the physical world. The nature of reality at the sub-atomic level forces physicists to acknowledge the difference from the macroscopic. They have to recognize the characteristics, however peculiar, of a self-subsistent reality. If, indeed, it is suggested that such things as photons and electrons do not have a 'natural subsistence nor are distinct from being perceived by any mind whatsoever' (as Berkeley puts it), it is hard to see what physics is investigating or *what* has forced physicists to change their minds and develop their theories. Old-fashioned philosophical prejudices sometimes incline physicists to the view that they need not care about anything beyond measurements. Even when we try to refer to something underlying the measurements, it is apparently very difficult to separate certain characteristics of what is measured from the act of measurement. Yet what possesses these characteristics? We can talk of spin, or angular momentum, and of other measurable quantities. We can agonize over whether the entities being investigated should be described as particles, or waves, or perhaps a combination of the two. Yet this all presupposes that there is *something* there putting limits on what we can reasonably say. Indeed the feeling that our previous concepts are inadequate in the face of new and stranger discoveries is unaccountable unless we realize that we are faced with something which is independent of mind. We are confronted with occurrences which we often cannot comprehend fully, but which force us to turn from the familiar concepts of classical physics. Perhaps the attractions of idealism have loomed large for some physicists because of their difficulty in explaining some puzzling features of external reality. They are not just acting on some philosophical whim but are being constrained by the difficulties they encounter when accounting for the results of their investigations at the sub-atomic level. Their penchant for idealism can be explained by the truth of realism.

The success of quantum mechanical formalism in prediction might lead us to expect that physical situations would correspond to its features. Yet, as in the case of Schrödinger's cat, it seems to make us talk about some very peculiar physical states. Some physicists[27] speculate that physical systems could be in mixed states corresponding to the various possible outcomes of measurement. This is difficult to comprehend. How could a system be in several conflicting states at once? Yet, however puzzling it may be to think of physical reality like this, at least it is right to try to discover its nature. This is the fundamental issue, and we should not shirk the problem by retreating to talk of scientific operations or of human consciousness. Einstein referred to one of the paradoxical aspects of quantum mechanics at the end of the paper written with Podolski and Rosen. They pointed out[28] that two systems can react with each other, be isolated from each other and yet still function as a combined system. If the state of the two systems were known before the interaction, we can calculate the state of the combined system at any later time. We cannot calculate the state in which either system is left. This can only be done with the help of further measurements. The point is, though, that when we have measured a particular quantity of the first system, such as its momentum, we can say with certainty what the momentum of the second system is. The same applies if we choose to measure, say, its position instead. In each case, the second system is held to be left in a different state. The authors say:

> We see therefore that as a consequence of two different measurements performed upon the first system, the second system may be left in states with two different wave functions. On the other hand, since at the time of measurement the two systems no longer interact, no real change can take place in the second system in consequence of anything that may be done to the first system. This is, of course, merely a statement of what is meant by the absence of an interaction between the two systems. Thus, *it is possible to assign two different wave functions . . . to the same reality* (the second system after the interaction with the first).

The measurement made on the first system appears to affect the second, if we conclude that the wave function gives an accurate description of reality. Different wave functions ought to entail that the reality they purport to describe is different. Yet, as Einstein points out, it goes against our usual (i.e. classical) notions of physical reality to conclude that the second system can be affected by the measurement we make on the first. He concludes that the wave function cannot change, because of something done to another isolated system.

Other examples of a similar problem can be produced from quantum mechanics. For instance, spin- and polarization-correlation experiments also indicate that the state of a physically isolated system (an atom) can be affected by a choice of measurement on another physical system which previously interacted with it. If we set out to measure the spin in one direction in the first system, quantum mechanics holds that we shall find a definite value and that, were we to measure the spin of the second system in the same direction, we should find it equal and opposite to the spin found in the first. Yet, if we decided to measure the spin found in different directions, we should also find the second system displayed an equal and opposite spin in these directions. The difficulty is summarized as follows:[29]

> Since the spins in the other directions must then be indeterminate, it is difficult to resist the conclusion that by changing our minds about which measurement to make on one of the systems, we are able to alter the state of the other system, from one in which its spin is definite in the z direction and indeterminate in the x and y directions, to one where it is definite in, say, the x direction and indeterminate in the y and z directions.

How can the action of a measuring instrument on one state bring the state of an isolated system into agreement with it? Such a state of affairs certainly strikes at the root of the assumptions of classical physics. It is not surprising that physicists have been tempted to duck the problem by refusing to face awkward questions about the nature of a reality that seems to behave like this. Hooker's comment is that 'one wants not a formal explanation of the situation, but a *physical* account of how it comes about'. He says that 'one wants the situation to be made physically plausible'.

Einstein's conviction that it was not at all plausible led him to doubt the satisfactoriness of quantum mechanics as it stood. His may not have been the correct reaction. Our understanding of the physical world, at least at a fundamental level, may need to be changed. The representation of interacting states given by quantum mechanics certainly leads to the view that one state can be affected by what happens to another, without there apparently being any physical mechanism to explain the correlation.

Quantum mechanics has been strikingly successful in predicting a wide variety of phenomena: its abstract formalism seems to be well established. Its interpretation, and in particular the way it describes reality, is still hotly disputed. Even if the reality of sub-atomic entities is conceded, there is still the question how far they possess measurable quantities apart from the process of measurement. Many difficulties have arisen because it is assumed that sub-atomic reality must conform to the concepts of classical physics. Once we admit that it might not, we are cast adrift in uncharted oceans. Such a plight may be uncomfortable, and even harrowing, but it is surely preferable to the pretence that the oceans are not there. The belief that there is a world independent of our conceptions of it inevitably carries with it in the possibility that we may at times be confronted with a reality which is, at least for the moment, beyond our comprehension. Discoveries in astrophysics, such as 'black holes' bear out this conclusion. The so-called 'immutable' laws of physics no longer apply in such areas. Physicists now entertain the possibility of the collapse of space-time, even though all laws of physics require space-time for their statement. Wheeler[30] talks of the possibility of total gravitational collapse 'whether big bang or black hole or big stop' and says:

> It is not the matter alone that collapses. With the collapse of space and time the framework falls down for everything one ever called a law of physics. Not law but mutability has the last word . . . The physics seems to

cry out, 'Find a way to state each law that lets that law fade from being.'

Yet this does not make gravitational collapse impossible or inconceivable to physicists. Reality is indeed far stranger than our developing conceptions of it may at any one time suggest.

7 KNOWLEDGE AND REALITY

Is Realism an Empirical Hypothesis?

One moral which we can draw from the previous chapter is that physical reality may at times be inexplicable in terms of our current conceptual framework. This conclusion has often seemed unpalatable, on the grounds that it seems 'metaphysical'. The more we remove reality from our grasp, the more 'transcendent' it seems to become. Yet we have seen that even material reality at the fundamental level does not appear to behave according to our expectations. There seems little reason why it should, since our expectations are formed by our experience of the behaviour of *macroscopic* objects. We must be wary of resting content with any current conceptual framework. We may not be able to possess detailed criteria about when to change or modify our concepts, but we are forced to look again at their adequacy when, as in quantum mechanics or astrophysics, we may be suddenly faced with phenomena which cannot be accounted for with our familiar concepts. Since they are *ex hypothesi* beyond the reach of our current scheme, one difficulty is that it will be very hard even to describe them properly. This point is sometimes used by those who argue that we must comprehend everything in terms of that scheme and that what is not comprehensible can be swept aside, on the grounds that any reference to 'it' must be meaningless. Yet at times the incomprehensible and the inconceivable reveal limitations in our understanding. To argue otherwise is to uphold an anthropocentricity which may satisfy man's ego, but does not reflect his true place in the universe. Man is *not* the measure of all things.

We may still feel that there must be a general connection between reality and what can be known. Yet reference to the possibility of knowledge must, if it means anything, take account of human capabilities and limitations. We cannot assume that these are ever likely to allow man to know everything. The possibility of full knowledge may serve as a goal and a challenge, but it may be a goal we never reach. If, though, knowledge increases and gets nearer it, we should expect a convergence of belief. We may be told that truth is many-sided or that reality has many aspects, but in science and in any other discipline with aspirations to truth, true beliefs should still be acceptable to all men. This may seem a statement of the obvious, but it can be very tempting to acquire a tolerance which allows that there is much truth and insight in many conflicting positions. It might even be held that no single position could include all insights and that a piece of knowledge could legitimately be rejected. Pluralism of this kind may assert the objectivity of what is known, but it fails to stress that there is only one way in which reality can be fully known. It becomes indistinguishable, as a result, from positions which deny the objectivity of reality and make what counts as reality internal to different systems.

Comparative religion provides an example of an area where sometimes the objectivity of what is known is claimed along with a refusal to acknowledge that any one religion could have complete knowledge of what is the case. This is not the same question as whether any religion actually *is* totally true and does not need to learn anything from others. What is being suggested is that no religion could ever achieve that position even by taking over the relevant insights of others. The possibility of convergence of beliefs in religion is being denied, just as it is being claimed that no one religion could ever be totally true. Some insights might be, it is thought, mutually exclusive but equally valid. Yet the proponents of this position face a problem. If what knowledge purports to be of exists independently and is not a mere projection from human belief, it must have a definite character. Religious believers claim knowledge of God even though He may be transcendent and genuinely above full human comprehension. The realist will not be worried by this, since much of the nature of the physical world lies beyond our conceptual understanding. Yet the definite character of God surely entails that He would have no contradictory attributes. The failure of any conceptual system to grasp His reality fully does not give a licence to different systems to diverge with impunity. Each may be trying to capture what they cannot fully capture, but their failure is a reflection of their own limitations. In this case, as in any other, the nature of reality entails that disagreement and divergence in beliefs means that at least one is wrong, and not knowledge. Divergence is a sign, if not of positive error, then at least of some deficiency. We need hardly add that mere convergence of belief is not a sufficient condition of truth.

The convergence of belief is often cited in science as a necessary consequence of the truth of realism. The existence of an external constraint on belief should eventually bring different beliefs into line. As scientists' investigations proceed, errors should be discovered, and in consequence eventual agreement arrived at (assuming they are perfectly rational). In addition, as science progresses, later theories must preserve the insights of earlier ones, whilst demonstrating their limitations. It is therefore sometimes argued that the further science is developed, building on the foundation of earlier theories, the greater the chance they have of being true. This view does not make any reference to an ideal limit, but is a straightforward empirical hypothesis. Putman says:[1]

> That science succeeds in making many true predictions, devising better ways of controlling nature, etc. is an undoubted empirical fact. If realism is an *explanation* of this fact, realism must itself be an over-arching scientific *hypothesis*. And realists have often embraced this idea, and proclaimed that realism *is* an empirical hypothesis.

This looks rather startling at first. Could realism be proved wrong by scientists? Putnam's point is that it could be, at least in the area of physical science, if science is shown to be a random succession of different theories positing different entities, rather than a developing discipline replacing earlier descriptions about, for example, electrons with more sophisticated ones. Realism may seem useless as an explanation of scientific success, if progress in science is an illusion, and within a century no term now used to refer by physicists will still be used. There would, it seems, be no success to explain. Yet this view itself presupposes that if scientific knowledge is attainable at all, we have at least partially attained it. This may seem plausible, but it would be open for someone faced with the total repudiation of twentieth-century physics in, say, the twenty-first century, to hold that twentieth-century scientists were just mistaken, and that science had in fact progressed. He could explain the repudiation of *our* physics by appealing to the very notions of objective truth and falsity which underly realism. Our commitment to our present scientific beliefs may be justified and we may possess knowledge, but it is no part of the realist's position to maintain that anyone is infallible. We cannot always know that we have knowledge, and total error need not undermine realism. Indeed, it can only be classed as *error* if realism is true and there *is* an independent world which we are trying unsuccessfully to refer to. Radical upheavals in science need not undermine realism, because it can be held that they occur when earlier mistakes are uncovered. Only the realist can maintain there is purpose in the upheaval.

The basic worry about the possibility that we may even now be making serious errors in our science is not one about the status of realism. No empirical discovery can affect realism because, whatever it is, the very idea of discovery presupposes the very concept of objective truth which the realist holds so dear. Without any reality, there is nothing to discover. The realist in fact must claim that so far from putting forward an empirical thesis, he is laying bare the most basic presuppositions of our thought and langauge. The basic worry in all this, in fact, is the fear of scepticism. If even apparently well-established physical theories, with a good record of success in prediction, are totally wrong, why should we ever think that knowledge of reality is attainable? Realism seems to be opening up too wide a gap between beliefs and reality, and by allowing plenty of room for the possibility of mistake it can easily undermine any confidence we have in our beliefs. Yet it is irrational to start doubting without good reason. The mere possibility that we may be mistaken does not mean that we are. The mere fact that realism allows a place for error, even when it is unrecognized, should be a spur to make us test our beliefs stringently, and to look at beliefs which differ from ours with a degree of tolerance. They may be right while ours are wrong.

The only alternative to a position which sometimes appears to allow scope for scepticism is one which rules out the possibility of wide-ranging error. Such a view may be very comforting, but it will ultimately have to come to terms with the bewildering variety of beliefs which men have held. If none of them is thought fundamentally mistaken, there is no possibility left of talking of mistake, or, conversely, of truth. When error is impossible, any belief or theory is as good as any other and it does not matter which one holds. In the world of ideas, at least, the permissive society soon becomes a nihilistic one. If it matters what we believe, we have to face that the price of possibly being right is that we could be wrong.

Realism is surely applicable to our scientific beliefs if it is applicable to any. Yet it seems rather curious to try to show that it is a contingent thesis, the truth of which depends on whether the terms of our present theories do for the most part actually refer to the entities they are intended to. It seems that realism is true if they do refer, and disproved if they do not. Yet the latter case is not so simple. If our theories are said to fail in their attempts to refer to particular entities, because the entities do not in fact exist, this may disprove the theories, but it *upholds* realism. It is not possible to envisage testing the claim of theories against reality, if realism is false, since reality would then only be what theories say it is. In other words, the fate of realism cannot be decided by 'success' or 'failure' in science, since the normal sense of these terms presupposes realism.

G. Maxwell makes the truth of scientific realism depend on the fate of scientific theories. He says :[2]'Realism is true if and only if it is contingently true that the unobservable entities like those referred to by scientific theories exist and false if they do not.'

All scientific questions about what exists are of course contingent, and any entities referred to by a theory may not exist. The truth of the theory demands that they should and the theory is disproved if it is found that they do not. Since the purpose of realism is to assert the self-subsistence of entities and deny that they are logically linked with obser-vation or any conceptual scheme, their fate does not in any way prove or disprove realism. Realism insists on their independence if they exist, but if they do not, this merely reinforces the view that what is the case and what is thought to be are logically distinct. Nevertheless, perhaps, Maxwell has hit on something important. Is not realism, it could be asked, at least committed to the view that *something* exists independently of scientific theories? Since existence is contingent, does not this mean that realism depends on the contingent fact of existence? Particular theories could be wrong in their claims about reality, but realism might seem in jeopardy if *all* theories were shown to be mistaken in their postulation of entities. Maxwell himself mentions unobserv-able entities, but realism is not just concerned with them, even though its distinctive claims, compared with posi-tivism, come out very clearly when it is willing to counte-nance such things. Any observable entity is just as self-subsistent. It does not exist *because* it can be observed.

The contingency of whatever exists may still appear to infect the realist's position. Could realism be contingent after all? We have to ask what would disprove realism, and whether the falsity of realism when applied to science would be demonstrated if we found that nothing existed, or at least nothing with which science concerns itself. This may seem an incredible discovery, and in it we are in fact questioning the reality of the material world. There would be no physical reality if *nothing* existed for science to study. This is not a self-contradictory notion, but we are talking about realism applied to science and there would be no science if there were no physical reality. What seems to be put at risk is not realism, but science. Of course there could be no so-called 'scientific realism' if there could be no science, but that is a tautology. Scientific realism is a contingent thesis because science itself is a contingent matter. Apart from the obvious point that it needs contingent beings to practise it, even as an abstract discipline viewed apart from the behaviour of scientists, it is necessarily concerned with contingent entities. Without a physical world, scientific realism would be false.

This brings us to the claim that if all entities, physical or not, are contingent, realism itself could still be false if there was *nothing*, and this would be a contingent falsity. How far existence might be necessary rather than contingent has long been a vexed question, but it certainly would seem strange if any question about the contingency of realism depended on whether some entities possess necessary existence. Their existence is self-subsistent if they necessarily exist, but even if we ignore them and accept that all existence is contingent existence, does this thereby make realism a contingent thesis? In that case, no object which does exist need have existed, and one day most entities currently existing will do so no longer. Might realism be true now but one day become false? The oddity of this question should be obvious, since the realist is not talking of particular entities. The strength of realism is that it is completely neutral about what does exist, but puts forward a view about the status of *whatever* does happen to exist. Such a position would still be valid even if nothing did, as it would still be true to say that whatever might exist, in addition to anyone's conceptions, would exist independently of them.

Realism can still entertain the possibility of existence even if there were nothing. Of course, one may doubt the coherence of the notion that nothing exists, and the view that nothing might exist seems more plausible. This indeed is just reasserting a belief in the contingency of all things. There might be nobody left to assert realism, if everything came to an end, but its truth as a doctrine about existence would be unaffected. If nothing existed, realism could still emphasize the self-subsistence of anything which was to come into existence. A parallel point can be made about idealism. Its truth could not be a contingent matter, depending on the fact that nothing except ideas happened to exist. Even if such a state of affairs were itself logically possible, there would still be a divergence between the idealist and the realist over the logical relationship of entities which might sometime exist and our conceptions of them. In fact the idealist would be unable to distinguish that situation from the earlier one where only ideas existed. The very notion that objects might not exist, although 'ideas' do, is itself a realist one.

Existence and Knowledge

What exists is in no way dependent on what man experiences or any conceptual scheme he may have. Put like this, one of the basic claims of what we have termed the 'realist' seems harmless and even banal. Yet a holder of a verification theory of truth would have to deny it. All knowledge would for him have to be formulated in empirically verifiable propositions and as Ayer once said,[3] 'all such propositions are to be incorporated in the system of empirical propositions which constitutes science'. Science is made the arbiter of truth, and, what is more, it is a science concerned ultimately with man's experience of the world, rather than the world itself. Ayer's treatment of the concept of God is typical. He refuses to allow that anyone could legitimately go beyond the occurrence of certain phenomena to talk of God. When, for instance, someone is impressed by the regularity he sees in nature and wants to conclude this is evidence of the existence of a Creator, Ayer would refuse to allow that what he says means anything more than that men have certain experiences. He says:[4] 'If the sentence "God exists" entails no more than that certain types of phenomena occur in certain sequences, then to assert the existence of a god will be simply equivalent to asserting that there is the requisite regularity in nature.'

He objected to a believer claiming that he was talking about a transcendent being 'who might be known through certain manifestations' on the grounds that 'in that case the term "god" is a metaphysical term'. Ayer refused utterly to go beyond what can be experienced. Everything has to be reduced to empirical terms. At the very beginning of *Language, Truth and Logic* he criticizes[5] 'the metaphysical thesis that philosophy affords us knowledge of a reality transcending the world of science and common sense'. He talks a few lines later of knowledge of 'a reality which transcended the phenomenal world' as if the 'phenomenal world' was a synonym for 'the world of science'. Yet we have already seen that the world of science may have to include entities that are unobservable, and hence not phenomenal. The step from empirical manifestations to underlying entity in physics is as great as the step from the possible empirical manifestations of God to the reality of God. Either step may or may not be justified, but the realist wishes to emphasize that justification ultimately depends on the nature of reality rather than on some philosophical position.

Many are alienated by this willingness to entertain the possibility of 'metaphysical' or 'transcendental' entities. They operate with some such premiss as that physical reality can be the only reality. This may be a reasonable assumption but it has to be argued on its merits. Indeed, if 'metaphysical' merely means what lies beyond the phenomenal world, many supposedly physical entities are thereby rendered metaphysical. The result is that a rigid empiricist will not allow reference to what lies beyond our experience in the material world even though its continuing existence would *explain* our experience. The rejection of the concept of a transcendent deity is made on the same basis as the rejection of any idea of unobservable material entities. This makes the rigid empiricist view of religion less challenging, since it seems highly inadequate even in explaining physics. It may be pointed out that our inability to experience parts of the physical world may be the result of a temporary limitation, and that more sophisticated experimental devices may make observable what was previously unobservable. There seems more of an obstacle to the view that one day we might obtain direct experience of the reality of God. Even here, though, the apparent distinction between the two cases may well rest on the fact that in the one we are dealing with physical reality and we just assume that that is more accessible. This may be so, but we must be careful not to rule out the possibility of experiencing non-physical reality without making the reason we are doing so very explicit.

Because we live in a material world, our concepts are conditioned by the physical circumstances with which we are familiar. There will always be difficulties over how we can comprehend any non-physical entity. The realist can, however, distinguish between what might exist and what we can understand. The snag is that we are sometimes not in a very good position to say anything meaningful about what lies mostly beyond our comprehension. Arguments have raged over the meaningfulness of the word 'God'. If we have no access to what the term refers to, it seems somewhat beside the point to suppose that there could be some deity of which we are totally unaware. We certainly would be in no position to say anything about it. In fact any religion has to show how we are in a position to speak about a transcendent god. Even though a god's existence may not depend on our ability to conceptualize, from the point of view of relevance to human life, a god about which nothing can be said is not much different from no god at all. The notion of revelation is important. If God exists, He has to reveal himself in ways which human beings can grasp for them to believe in Him. In the specific case of Christianity, the doctrine of the

Incarnation, where God is said to have become man, attempts to explain how a transcendent God could show Himself in a way which man could understand. Nevertheless, His reality would not be limited to what can be experienced, even if what man could say about Him was restricted. Once again, the distinction between man's conceptual understanding and what the understanding is of is crucial.

The refusal to dismiss out of hand the existence of entities beyond our experience may make us less dogmatic in saying what can be experienced. The curious thing about many empiricists is that they are not just content to emphasize the role our experience plays in building up our theory of the world, but wish to place limits on what we might expect to experience. Ayer maintained in *Language, Truth and Logic* that a proposition which could not be empirically verified could not be a genuine proposition. Yet the kind of empirical verification he found acceptable consisted of tests by a scientist of the time, and he ruled out many experiences which science could not account for. He criticized the mystic, for example, and said of him:[6] 'The fact that he cannot . . . even himself devise an empirical test to validate his "knowledge" shows that his state of mystical intuition is not a genuinely cognitive state.' I am not going to discuss the merits and demerits of mysticism, but it is noteworthy that *if* the mystic were genuinely experiencing some non-physical reality, he could not devise an 'empirical' test to validate his experience. 'Empirical' is in fact used by Ayer not just to cover what can be experienced, but to refer to the possible experience of *material* reality, as studied by science.

The realist who is not a materialist will keep an open mind on what could exist. He may well conclude sometimes that some putative entities do not exist, but he will exclude nothing until he has looked at the merits of the particular case. Our judgements should ideally be governed by and conform to what there is. Certainly, reality will not alter merely so as to conform to our judgements. Yet, although knowledge should be our goal, we have seen that it is dangerous to assume that human limitations can be swept aside as of no account. What can be known may be only part of what there is. The suggestion that reality partly consists in lying open to being known may seem a challenge to this, and we may still feel that there is something odd about an entity which cannot be known. Does it not follow from its very existence that one would be able to acknowledge it if one were not subject to whatever limitations constrain us? The notion of omniscience surely involves some such thought. We may, for instance, think in terms of some imaginary superman, not subject to the bounds normally restraining man.

Omniscience is generally thought a property of God, and it is natural to suppose that all things are known by Him (if He exists). Does it follow that a property of reality is that it is known by God? That would certainly close the gap between reality and knowledge, so that what exists not only can be known but *is* known, at least by God. This way of putting it may not seem so very far from Berkeley's notion of reality depending on being perceived by God. There is, however, a great deal of difference between saying that God's omniscience entails that He knows everything and saying that everything exists because God knows it. In the former case, reality does not consist in being known by Him. He knows it *because* it is real. There is the further question about how far everything causally depends on Him in his role as Creator. He can create or destroy at will, if He is omnipotent, but this does not cast doubt on the self-subsistent reality of Creation. Indeed, the concept of Creation surely entails that something is created which has a reality apart from its Creator. It may be causally dependent on Him in many ways, but its reality is not logically dependent on Him. Its existence is a genuine one and it is ontologically separate from its Creator. It is possible to accept its existence and deny that of any Creator without contradiction. If there is a God, the universe He created can be said to exist in just the same way as He does. The differences between them do not stem from any different kind of reality possessed by either, but from the fact that God and physical reality each have different characteristics. God is not a material object.

We cannot define reality in terms of knowledge, whether that of God or of some future generation of scientists. It would not be knowledge if it was not accurate, but so far from knowledge creating reality, there would be nothing to know if nothing existed. This way of putting it may suggest that knowledge is merely a passive reflection of a static reality, but, in fact, questions of how far reality changes or is static are irrelevant. Those concern its nature and proper knowledge will include a full understanding of that, whatever form it may take. Questions about activity or passivity in knowing are more complicated. Full knowledge must indeed reflect the definite nature of reality, but the role of selection in describing features of reality is important. This, though, does not prove that, whether through the medium of our minds, our concepts, or our language, we play an active role in moulding the world. It merely shows that when confronted with the multifarious aspects of reality, we often pick out the features relevant to our present purposes, and ignore the rest.

One mark of reality which is sometimes mentioned is its resistance to our will. What lies beyond us is not always under our control. We can change what we think or imagine something different at will, but the outside world, whether in the form of other people or ordinary material objects, is not so amenable to manipulation. Sometimes we can control it and often we cannot. The world does not always conform to our judgements and beliefs and this has doubtless contributed to the view that we are the passive recipients of information about an outside world. We do gain knowledge of 'something there' which cannot be easily moulded to suit our whims. There is, however, a sense in which our knowledge may always be relative, since it is limited by the categories of thought available to us and by opportunities we may have for extending it. The knowledge we have *is* knowledge, but it is partial. This is seen very clearly in the context of science where the insights of one theory, if genuine ones, have to be retained by all subsequent theories, although they may be put in a different context. Quantum mechanics can never replace classical mechanics at the level of macroscopic objects, and its findings must always be consistent with the proven predictions of classical mechanics at the level that it was designed to deal with. Classical mechanics cannot be applied to the level of the microscopic. Its discoveries were valid but could not be generalized to cover every set of circumstances. Talk of 'relative' knowledge merely spotlights the fact that this kind of limitation often reduces the scope of our understanding, whether or not we realize it at the time. Yet our understanding *is* still correct, since partial, or relative, knowledge is knowledge, and the mere use of the term 'relative' need not make us fear that we are lapsing into the kind of position which makes truth and reality themselves relative matters. 'Relative' is in fact being opposed to 'absolute' rather than 'objective'. Recognition of our limitations should not cast doubt in any way on the objectivity of reality.

Conclusion

One fear which many have when confronted with such labels as 'scientific realism' is that in some way humanity is being ignored. This is a difficult objection to state with any rigour, but there is no doubt that an insistence on objectivity and an attack on anthropocentricity make many feel that men are being left out of the reckoning. Men sometimes seem to become the servants rather than the masters of science and techonology. This is a genuine worry, but it is totally irrelevant to the questions we have been considering. Labels such as 'scientific realism' are sometimes used as a belligerent war-cry in favour of science at any cost. Yet the mere insistence that we separate the subject from the object of knowledge, and recognize that human knowledge is not necessarily coextensive with reality is a completely neutral thesis when we look for wider implications. Asserting that reality-for-us is not to be identified with reality-in-itself, and that ontology cannot be reduced to epistemology, implies nothing about men and their priorities.

In fact, when men make rational judgements about the nature of reality, even though they cannot be said to create it, they are taking part in a distinctively human activity. Human rationality is put at risk more by those who would make truth inaccessible than by those who insist that man is not the measure of all things. It is a paradox that man can demand the centre of the stage, insisting that everything should depend on him, and yet in the end find that in doing so he has lost his rationality and his freedom. Realism takes the possibility of error and ignorance seriously, but it also gives men the chance of notable successes in extending the range of their understanding. It gives them something to reason about, while acknowledging that they are free to make mistakes. The removal of the possibility of error may make man's judgements part of some wider process, perhaps a social one, but it also separates them from any shadow of rationality. Without objective reality, we can say nothing true, and without the possibility of truth and error, there can be no possibility of rational judgement. Without rationality, men can have no freedom of choice. The notion of strong objectivity does not force men into some inhuman mould, but is a precondition for everything which has traditionally been thought to be distinctively human. It is significant that once men's reality is emphasized at the expense of reality-in-itself, it seems natural to look for explanations why anyone should think that reality is like that. Yet sociological and psychological explanations are themselves only valid on realist assumptions, since an assault on the possibility of any discovery of truth undermines the point of all human intellectual activity. The path from various anti-realist positions to solipsism and nihilism is often surprisingly short.

It is all very well, we may be told, uttering stark warnings of the terrible consequences of repudiating a realist view of truth. Even if they are justified, how does that help anyone here and now? Doctrines of truth are beside the point, it may be claimed, since what is needed is advice on how to arrive at truth and avoid error. Metaphysics, and ontology, may provide goals for human reason, and scientists may recognize that their work is based on the presupposition that reality is discovered and not created. What difference does this make in the actual choices they make between theories? It seems that we need a methodology rather than mere exhortations about the need to discover what is real. Given two theories, how should we decide which provides a path to truth? When confronted with rival conceptual systems, what criteria can be employed to choose the one which is more likely to reflect reality?

These are important questions. The search for a methodology is crucial in the philosophy of science. Nevertheless, a methodology itself presupposes that there is a purpose in choosing one method rather than another. The epistemological anarchism advocated by some becomes inevitable once the notion of an independent reality is rejected. Consideration of methodology will only beg important questions, until there is agreement about the fundamental goal, and indeed until it is recognized that there *is* a goal. There can, too, be no overall prescription for arriving at knowledge of reality, since it all depends what part of reality is being investigated. A lot of the discussion over what it is rational to believe has been bedevilled in the last few decades by the assumption that the methods appropriate for the discovery of truth in the natural sciences are essential everywhere. It has to easily been thought that if we cannot discover, say, God or moral truth by scientific means, we cannot talk of truth in religion or morality. Indeed, it has too easily been assumed that we know the right methodology even for science.

'Reality' is not some monolithic absolute to which there is only one path. There is no unique set of all-purpose criteria which will help us to discover what is the case in any area, whether it be physics or theology. The very natures of the objects of our interest should dictate different strategies to uncover them. This may seem a somewhat negative conclusion. The mere distinction between the subject and object of possible knowledge does not go very far in telling us what kind of objects we can gain knowledge of, or indeed *how* we can gain knowledge. A feeling of frustration at being refused help here and now has in fact led many to eschew anything 'metaphysical'. Peirce's desire to start from where we are, the empiricist's wish to stick with observations, or the repudiation by many of unknowable things-in-themselves in favour of reality-for-us, are all symptoms of an urge to become concrete and deal with man's actual epistemological problems. The switch of interest from the content to the fact of belief is another result of the desire to be concrete and specific rather than metaphysical and general. In one sense, of course, we have to start from where we are, and it is precisely because we have no definite knowledge of where we are going until we get there, that detailed prescriptions for the right route are always going to be impossible. When we are confronted with difficult and apparently competing conceptual systems, we may know that one at least must be mistaken without being in a position to say which. The error made by many philosophers is to conclude that the whole concept of mistake and objective reality is useless and must be discarded. Travel along an unknown route to an unknown destination becomes pointless if we conclude there *is* no destination.

Another major error which philosophers have often made is to oppose concepts and reality in such a way that reality is somehow always beyond reach. Our concepts may be mistaken or inadequate, but they may also be quite correct in the distinctions they draw. Reality may be as we say it is, and we may be drawing attention to real similarities and differences. On the everyday level this is what makes the teaching and learning of language possible. We may not be always in a position to stand back from ourselves and *say* that we possess knowledge, but we may well have it. The success of modern scientists in manipulating the world could be accidental, but it is more likely to be the result of their growing understanding of what the material world is really like. Much of reality *is* accessible.

'Reality' has often been used by philosophers as a term to describe the ineffable and transcendent. I have not done this. Although its apparent abstraction may make it look as if some mysterious 'Absolute' is being invoked, this is far from being so. We are trying to refer to reality whenever we say what we think exists. Some may wish to talk of God, and others may think matter is the ultimate reality. Nevertheless, we all talk about tables and chairs, cats and rabbits. They exist, and are real, and do not just depend in some way on our thought for their existence. The rabbithood of a rabbit is not just the result of some whim on the part of a biologist thinking up a theory. The same can be said of sub-atomic particles, although here the issues are more controversial.

Man himself is a part of reality, and causally interacts with other segments of reality. He can change things, and even sometimes control them. He does not decide what is real and what is not, but he can make up his mind what he thinks real. This is the pursuit of truth. Man's attempt to make true assertions about the self-subsistent world of which he is a part may not always be successful, and may not always prove easy or straightforward. The repudiation of it as a goal would not only destroy science, but would make human intellectual activity totally pointless.

NOTES TO TEXT

Introduction

1 'The Scientific Conception of the World: The Vienna Circle' reprinted in *Otto Neurath : Empiricism and Sociology*, M. Neurath and R. S. Cohen (eds.), p. 306ff.
2 S. W. Hawking: 'Breakdown of Predictability in Gravitational Collapse', *Physical Review*, D. 14, no. 10 (1976), pp. 2460ff.
3 Cf. my *Reason and Commitment*, p. 8f.
4 H. Mehan and H. Wood, *The Reality of Ethnomethodology*, p. 68.
5 Op. cit. p. 37.
6 Op. cit. p. 114.
7 See *Reason and Commitment*, p. 99ff.
8 Roy Bhaskar, *A Realist Theory of Science*, p. 36.
9 Op. cit. p.249.
10 *The Principles of Genetic Epistemology*, W. Mays (trans.), p. 88.
11 Op. cit. p. 82.
12 *Experience and the Growth of Understanding*, p. 59.
13 I. Dilman, 'Universals: Bambrough on Wittgenstein'. *Proceedings of the Aristotelian Society*, LXXIX (1978–9), p. 50.
14 'Reality without Reference' *Dialectica*, 31 (1977), p. 253.

1

1 *Essay concerning Human Understanding*, A. S. Pringle Patterson (ed.), p. 155.
2 *Conceptual Idealism*, p. 3.
3 Idem. p. 100.
4 Idem. p. 111.
5 Idem. p. 117.
6 Idem. p. 167.
7 Idem. p. 171.

8   *Philosophical Investigations,* § 304.
9   Idem. p. 165.
10 Idem. p. 154.
11 *Principles of Human Knowledge,* p. 108.
12 *Critique of Pure Reason,* preface to second edition, Kemp Smith (ed.), p. 22.
13 Idem. p. 273.
14 *Collected Papers,* 8.12.
15 Idem. 5.494.
16 Idem. 5.409.
17 Idem. 5.494.
18 Idem. 5.416.
19 Idem. 8.12.
20 Idem. 5.416.
21 Idem. 2.135.
22 Idem. 8.12.
23 Idem. 8.16.
24 *Logic,* ch. 4, p. 13ff IB2 Box 8—quoted in Murphey, *Development of Peirce's Philosophy,* p. 167.

2

1   *Materialism and Empirio-Criticism,* p. 59.
2   Idem. p. 220.
3   Idem. p. 65.
4   Idem. p. 39.
5   Idem. p. 96.
6   Butts and Hintikka (eds.), *Historical and Philosophical Dimensions of Logic, Methodology and Philosophy of Science,* p. 195ff.
7   *Marxism and Materialism,* p. 5.
8   Idem. p. 65.
9   Idem. p. 79.
10 Idem. p. 108.
11 *A Rational Animal,* p. 217.
12 *Idealism,* p. 392.
13 *Materialism and Empirio-Criticism,* p. 265.
14 Idem. p. 222.
15 Idem. p. 240.
16 *Early Texts,* D. McLellan (ed.), p. 176.

17 For example by Z. A. Jordan in *Philosophy and Ideology*.
18 'Karl Marx and the Classical Definition of Truth', p. 66 in *Marxism and Beyond*.
19 Idem. p. 67.
20 Idem. p. 77.
21 Idem. p. 86.
22 *Frege*, p. 589.
23 Idem. p. 465.
24 'The Reality of the Past', *Proceedings of the Aristotelian Society*, LXIX (1968–9), p. 249.
25 'Truth', *Proceedings of the Aristotelian Society*, LIX (1958–9), p. 157.
26 *Proceedings of the Aristotelian Society*, LXIX (1968–9), p. 244.
27 'On "The Reality of the Past" ' in *Action and Interpretation*, Hookway and Pettit (eds.), p. 143.
28 Idem. p. 136.
29 Idem. p. 134.
30 'What is a Theory of Meaning? (11)' in *Truth and Meaning*, Evans and McDowell (eds.), p. 100.
31 'Scruton and Wright on Anti-Realism', *Proccdings of the Aristotelian Society*, LXXVII (1976–7), p. 21.
32 For a criticism of this tendency, see my 'Thought and Language', *Proceedings of the Aristotelian Society*, LXXIX (1978–9).
33 See my *Pain and Emotion*.
34 Cf. Wittgenstein, *Philosophical Investigations*, § 293.
35 Cf. H. Putnam, *Meaning and the Moral Sciences*, p. 26f.
36 Crispin Wright, 'Truth Conditions and Criteria', *Proceedings of the Aristotelian Society, Supplementary Volume*, L (1976), p. 226.
37 *Meaning and the Moral Sciences*, p. 29.
38 Idem. p. 20.

3

1 *The Essential Tension*, p. xxii.
2 *Against Method*, p. 30 (his italics).
3 Idem. p. 195.
4 Idem. p. 284 (his italics).

5 See C. A. Hooker, 'Systematic Realism', *Synthese*, 26 (1974), p. 420.
6 *The Physicist's Conception of Nature*, J. Mehra (ed.), p. 269.
7 Idem. p. 279.
8 'The Nature of Natural Knowledge', *Mind and Language*, S. Guttenplan (ed.), p. 81.
9 *Word and Object*, p. 23.
10 *Mind and Language*, p. 74.
11 *From a Logical Point of View*, p. 44.
12 *Word and Object*, p. 22.
13 'Replies', *Words and Objections, Essays on the Work of W. V. Quine*, p. 293.
14 *Word and Object* p. 22.
15 *Ontological Relativity*, p. 50.
16 Idem. p. 38.
17 *Ontological Relativity*, p. 80.
18 *Mind and Language*, p. 80.
19 Idem. p. 73.
20 See for example the work of S. Kripke and H. Putnam.
21 In discussion.
22 *Word and Object*, p. 24.
23 *Word and Object*, p. 39.
24 *Roots of Reference*, p.54.
25 *Meaning and the Moral Sciences*, p. 32.
26 *Ontological Relativity*, p. 82.
27 *Words and Objections*, p. 302.
28 *Mind and Language*, S. Guttenplan (ed.), p. 84.
29 Idem. p. 95.
30 *Word and Objections*, p. 303.
31 *Meaning and the Moral Sciences*, p. 50.
32 *Einstein*, Schilpp (ed.), p. 295.
33 Idem. p. 254.

4

1 'On the Very idea of a Conceptual Scheme', p. 12.
2 See my *Reason and Commitment*.
3 *Words and Objections*, Davidson and Hintikka (eds.), p. 92.
4 'Thought and Talk', *Mind and Language*, p. 14.
5 Idem. p. 21.

6 'Belief and the Basis of Meaning', *Synthese,* 27 (1974), p. 321.
7 *Meaning and the Moral Sciences,* p. 22ff.
8 'One the Very Idea of a Conceptual Scheme', p. 16.
9 'The World Well Lost', *Journal of Philosophy,* 69 (1972), p. 663.
10 Milton Fisk, 'The World Regained', *Journal of Philosophy,* 69(1972), p. 668.

5

1 Cf. *The Social Construction of Reality,* Berger and Luckmann, p. 15.
2 *Sociological Theory and Philosophical Analysis,* Emmett and MacIntyre (eds.), p. 4.
3 *History and Class Consciousness,* p. 19.
4 Idem. p. 149.
5 Idem. p. 180ff.
6 *Ideology and Utopia,* p. 256.
7 Idem. p. 135.
8 Idem. p. 267.
9 'Teaching and Learning as the Organization of Knowledge', G. M. Esland in *Knowledge and Control,* M. Young (ed.), p. 77.
10 'Man's Place in Nature' by R. Young in *Changing Perspectives in the History of Science,* M. Teich and R. Young (eds.), p. 429.
11 *History and Class Consciousness,* p. 234.
12 *The Sociology of Science,* p. 9.
13 Barry Barnes, *Scientific Knowledge and Sociological Theory,* p. 69.
14 Idem. p. 64.
15 *Against Method,* p. 166.
16 'Understanding Alien Belief Systems' in *British Journal of Sociology,* 20 (1969), p. 72.
17 David Bloor, *Knowledge and Social Imagery,* p. 5.
18 *Scientific Knowledge and Sociological Theory,* p. 154.
19 *Theaetetus* 201.

6

1 *Foundational Problems in the Special Sciences,* p. 27ff.
2 *Man and Science,* p. 46.
3 *Gravitation,* Misner, Thorne and Wheeler, p. 1217.

4 J. M. Jauch in *Foundations of Quantum Mechanics*, B. d'Espagnat (ed.), p. 21.
5 Idem. G. Prosperi, p. 97.
6 Idem. p. 122.
7 *Symmetries and Reflections*, p. 175.
8 Idem. p. 189.
9 *Americal Scientist*, 62 (1974), p. 690.
10 B. d'Espagnat in *The Physicist's Conception of Nature*, Mehra (ed.), p. 715.
11 Idem. p. 728.
12 *Einstein*, Schilpp (ed.), p. 209.
13 Idem. p. 217.
14 A. B. Pippard, in *Quanta and Reality*, p. 27.
15 *Einstein*, Schilpp (ed.), p. 260.
16 A. Einstein, N. Rosen and B. Podolski, *Physical Review*, 47, (1935), p. 777.
17 *Einstein*, Schilpp (ed.), p. 262.
18 Idem. p. 195.
19 *Foundations of Quantum Mechanics*, B. d'Espagnat (ed.), p. 173.
20 R. Haag in *The Physicist's Conception of Nature*, Mehra (ed.), p. 695.
21 Oral Comment quoted by A. Petersen in *Bull. Atom Sci.* 78 (1963), p. 12.
22 *The Physicist's Conception of Nature* Mehra (ed.), p. 744.
23 Idem. p. 656.
24 *Conceptual Foundations of Quantum Mechanics*, p. 301.
25 *Philosophical Papers, Mathematics, Matter and Method*, vol. 1, p. 152.
26 Idem. p. 157.
27 Cf. J. Jauch in *Foundations of Quantum Mechanics*.
28 *Physical Review*, 47 (1935), p. 779.
29 C. A. Hooker, *American Journal of Physics*, 38 (1970), p. 855.
30 *Foundational Problems in the Special Sciences*, Butts and Hintikka (eds.), p. 15.

7

1 *Meaning and the Moral Sciences*, p. 19.
2 *The Nature and Function of Scientific Theories*, R. G. Colodny (ed.), p. 11.

3 *Language, Truth and Logic,* p. 120.
4 Idem. p. 115.
5 Idem. p. 23.
6 Idem. P. 119.

BIBLIOGRAPHY (of works cited)

Ayer, A. J., *Language, Truth and Logic* (2nd edn), London 1946.

Barnes, B., *Scientific Knowledge and Sociological Theory*, London 1974.

Bell, J. S., 'Introduction to the Hidden Variable Question' in *Foundations of Quantum Mechanics*, B. d'Espagnat (ed.).

Berger, P. L. and Luckmann, T., *The Social Construction of Reality*, Harmondsworth 1971.

Berkeley, G., *Principles of Human Knowledge*, G. J. Warnock (ed.), London 1962.

Bhaskar, R., *A Realist Theory of Science* (2nd edn), Hassocks 1978.

Bloor, D., *Knowledge and Social Imagery*, London 1976.

Bohr, N., 'Discussion with Einstein on Epistemological Problems in Atomic Physics' in *Einstein*, P. Schilpp (ed.).

Butts, R. E. and Hintikka, J. (eds.), *Foundational Problems in the Special Sciences* (Part Two of the Proceedings of the Fifth International Congress of Logic, Methodology, and Philosophy of Science), Dordrecht 1977.
Historical and Philosophical Dimensions of Logic, Methodology and Philosophy of Science (Part Four of the above), Dordrecht 1977.

Colodny, R. G. (ed.), *The Nature and Function of Scientific Theories*, Pittsburgh 1970.

Davidson, D., 'On the Very Idea of a Conceptual Scheme', Presidential Address to the Eastern Meeting of the American Philosophical Association, December 1973.
'Belief and the Basis of Meaning', *Synthese*, 27 (1974).
'Thought and Talk' in *Mind and Language*, S. Guttenplan (ed.).

'Reality Without Reference', *Dialectica*, 31 (1977).

Dilman, I. 'Universals: Bambrough on Wittgenstein', *Proceedings of the Aristotelian Society*, LXXIX (1978–9).

Dummett, M., 'Truth', *Proceedings of the Aristotelian Society*, LIX (1958–9).

'The Reality of the Past', *Proceedings of the Aristotelian Society*, LXIX (1968–9).

Frege, London 1973.

'What is a Theory of Meaning? (II)' in *Truth and Meaning*, G. Evans and J. McDowell (eds.).

Einstein, A., Rosen, N. and Podolski, B., 'Can Quantum-Mechanical Description of Physical Reality Be Considered Complete', *Physical Review*, 47 (1935).

Emmett, D. and MacIntyre, A. (eds), *Sociological Theory and Philosophical Analysis*, London 1970.

Esland, G. M., 'Teaching and Learning as the Organization of Knowledge' in *Knowledge and Control*, M. F. D. Young (ed.).

d'Espagnat, B., *Conceptual Foundations of Quantum Mechanics*, California 1971.

(ed.) Foundations of Quantum Mechanics, New York 1971.

'Quantum Logic and Non-Separability' in *The Physicist's Conception of Nature*, J. Mehra (ed.).

Evans, G. and McDowell, J., *Truth and Meaning*, Oxford 1976.

Ewing, A. C., *Idealism*, London 1934.

Feyerabend, P., *Against Method*, London 1975.

Fisk, M., 'The World Regained', *Journal of Philosophy*, 69 (1972).

Flew, A. G. N., *A Rational Animal*, Oxford 1978.

Guttenplan, S. (ed.), *Mind and Language*, Oxford 1975.

Haag, R., 'Subject, Object and Measurement' in *The Physicist's Conception of Nature* J. Mehra (ed.).

Habermas, J., 'Knowledge and Interest' in *Sociological Theory and Philosophical Analysis*, D. Emmett and A. MacIntyre (eds.).

Hamlyn, D., *Experience and the Growth of Understanding*, London 1978.

Hawking, S. W., 'Breakdown of Predictability in Gravitational Collapse', *Physical Review*, D. 14 (1976).

Heitler, W., 'Departure from Classical Thought' in *Einstein* P. Schilpp (ed.).
Man and Science, London 1963.

Hooker, C. W., 'Concerning EPR's Objection to Quantum Theory', *American Journal of Physics*, 38 (1970).
'Systematic Realism', *Synthese*, 26 (1974).

Hookway, C. and Pettit, P. (eds.), *Action and Interpretation*, Cambridge 1978.

Jauch, J. M., *Foundations of Quantum Mechanics*, New York 1968.

Jordan, Z. A., *Philosophy and Ideology*, Dordrecht 1963.

Kant, I., *Critique of Pure Reason*, N. Kemp Smith (ed.), London 1929.

Kedrov, B. M., 'The Concept of Matter' in *Historical and Philosophical Dimensions of Logic, Methodology and Philosophy of Science*, R. Butts and J. Hintikka (eds.).

Kolakowski, L., *Marxism and Beyond*, J. Z. Peel (trans.), London 1968.

Kuhn, T., *The Structure of Scientific Revolutions*, Chicago 1962.
The Essential Tension, Chicago 1977.

Lenin, V., *Materialism and Empirio-Criticism*, London 1927. (Also published as vol. xiv of *Collected Works*, Moscow)

Locke, J., *Essay Concerning Human Understanding*, A. S. Pringle Patterson (ed.), Oxford 1924.

Lukacs, G., *History and Class Consciousness*, London 1971.

Mannheim, K., *Ideology and Utopia*, London 1936.

Margeneau, H., 'Einstein's Conception of Reality' in *Einstein*, P. Schilpp (ed.).

Marx, K., *Early Texts*, D. McLellan (ed.), Oxford 1971.

McDowell, J., 'On "The Reality of the Past" ' in *Action and Interpretation*, C. Hookway and P. Pettit (eds.).

Mehan, H. and Wood, H., *The Reality of Ethnomethodology*, New York 1975.

Mehra, J. (ed.), *The Physicist's Conception of Nature*, Dordrecht 1973.

Merton, R. K., *The Sociology of Science*, Chicago 1973.

Misner, C. W. Thorne, K. S. and Wheeler, J. A., *Gravitation*, San Francisco 1973.

Murphey, M. G., *The Development of Peirce's Philosophy*, Cambridge, Mass. 1961.

Neurath, M. and Cohen, R. S. (eds.), *Otto Neurath: Empiricism and Sociology*, Dordrecht 1973.

Peel, J. D. Y., 'Understanding Alien Belief Systems', *British Journal of Sociology*, 20 (1969).

Peirce, C. S., *Collected Papers*, vols. 1–8, Cambridge, Mass. 1931–58.

Petersen, A., 'The Philosophy of Niels Bohr', *Bulletin of Atomic Science*, 78 (1963).

Piaget, J., *The Principles of Genetic Epistemology*, W. Mays (trans.), London 1972.

Pippard, A. B., 'Particles and Waves' In *Quanta and Reality, A Symposium*, London 1962.

Prosperi, G. M., 'Macroscopic Physics and the Problem of Measurement in Quantum Mechanics', in *Foundations of Quantum Mechanics*, B. d'Espagnat (ed.).

Putnam, H., *Mathematics, Matter and Method: Philosophical Papers*, vol. 1, Cambridge 1975.

Meaning and the Moral Sciences, London 1978.

Quine, W. V., *Word and Object*, Cambridge, Mass. 1960.

From a Logical Point of View 2nd edn., New York 1963.

Ontological Relativity, New York 1969.

'Replies' in *Words and Objections: Essays on the Work of W. V. Quine*, Dordrecht 1969.

Roots of Reference, Illinois 1974.

'The Nature of Natural Knowledge' and 'Mind and Verbal Dispositions' in *Mind and Language*, S. Guttenplan (ed.).

Reichenbach, H., 'The Philosophical Significance of the Theory of Relativity' in *Einstein*, P. A. Schilpp (ed.).

Rescher, N., *Conceptual Idealism*, Oxford 1973.

Rorty, R., 'The World Well Lost', *Journal of Philosophy*, 69 (1972).

Ruben, D-H., *Marxism and Materialism*, Hassocks 1977.

Schilpp, P. A. (ed.), *Albert Einstein, Philosopher-Scientist*, Evanston, Illinois 1949.

Strawson, P., 'Scruton and Wright on Anti-Realism', *Proceedings of the Aristotelian Society*, LXXVII (1976–7).

Teich, M. and Young, R. (eds.), *Changing Perspectives in the History of Science*, London 1973.

Trigg, R., *Pain and Emotion*, Oxford 1970.

Reason and Commitment, Cambridge 1973.

'Thought and Language', *Proceedings of the Aristotelian Society* LXXIX (1978–9).

von Weizacker, C. F., 'Physics and Philosophy' and 'Classical and Quantum Descriptions' in *The Physicist's Conception of Nature*, J. Mehra (ed.).

Wheeler, J. A., 'The Universe as Home for Man', *American Scientist*, 62 (1974).

'Genesis and Observership' in *Foundational Problems in the Special Sciences*, R. E. Butts and J. Hintikka (eds.).

Wigner, E., *Symmetries and Reflections*, Bloomington, Indiana 1967.

Wittgenstein, L., *Philosophical Investigations*, Oxford 1958.

Wright, C., 'Truth Conditions and Criteria', *Proceedings of the Aristotelian Society, Supplementary Volume*, L (1976).

Young, M. F. D. (ed.), *Knowledge and Control*, London 1971.

Young, R., 'Man's Place in Nature' in *Changing Perspectives in the History of Science*, M. Teich and R. Young (eds.), London 1973.

INDEX

213